Unashamed

A Memoir of My Closet
Coming in and Coming Out

UNASHAMED: A MEMOIR OF MY CLOSET COMING IN AND COMING OUT

This is a memoir, names have been changed to protect people's privacy, any resemblance to actual events, locales, or persons, either living or dead, is purely coincidental.

Copyright ©2019 and © 2014 by Emma Janson

All rights reserved. No part of this book may be used or reproduced in any manner whatsoever without the prior written permission of the publisher, except in the case of brief quotations embodied in critical articles and reviews.

For more information, to inquire about rights to this or other works, or to purchase copies for special educational, business, or sales promotional uses please write to:

SECOND EDITION

Printed in the United States of America

Unashamed

A Memoir of My Closet
Coming in and Coming Out

Emma Janson

Dedication

I dedicate this book to those who find knowledge and advice within the mistakes I have made and others who are strictly entertained. May you laugh, learn and find peace in your own rainbow.

Ode

Ode to the mighty dry hump; the Godsend to any little girl's clitoral repertoire.

My sexual adventures began with mutual exploration and self-gratification. This lets me know there are others with freak tendencies. Thank you, friends, family, and girls who in their own prepubescent curiosities let me play humping games. After all, it was you who unintentionally led me to personal sexual discovery.

Thanks to all who lay beneath me under the Cabbage Patch sheet set re-enacting adult roles on cheesy seventies sitcoms. I played the role of Jack Tripper from Three's Company and you, the various women he tried to have sex with, including my favorite character, Lonna, the older sex-starved woman always throwing herself at Jack's feet. All she wanted was for Jack to *caress* her body, a word we copied and used over and over again as the Cabbage Patch kids covered our shame.

Bless you, for suggesting we brush our teeth before we practiced French kissing for the boys, for sneaking me into your mom's room to show me porn, and for letting me taste her edible underwear before cramming them back into the package half eaten.

Thank you, babysitter: for comforting me as tears wet my cheeks over my stubbed toe from a vigorous game of kick-the-can. The view of your ample teenage breasts peeking curiously from your sweater as you hugged me is an image timeless to this day. My ticket to hell may have been purchased for crying uncontrollably to get that second mesmerizing look.

Thank you, friends, for letting me sleep in your bed during a sleepover, rather than on the floor and for undressing in front of me proclaiming, "Who cares? We're both girls." Ladies, thank you because through the confusion of sexual identity you were always there to bring me back to the bosom of familiarity. Pun intended.

Unashamed

A Memoir of My Closet
Coming in and Coming Out

Chapter 1

Every person remembers their first crush. For me, there were a few before my world revolved around my first "girl" crush in the eighth-grade.

It literally began on the very first day of school. She was full of sunshine and rainbows from the moment our eyes met. When she smiled her brilliant teeth gleamed from cheek to freckled cheek, offset by a summer tan. She scanned the room and made a beeline for the empty seat next to me beaming when she asked if she could sit there. She had the biggest turquoise eyes that complimented her wide smile, freckles, and perfectly teased bangs. No one could refuse her when she smiled.

She pulled supplies from her pink and purple bag making eighth-grade small talk, "Isn't this exciting, the first day of class! How was your summer? Hi, I'm Sunny." Then she reached out her hand to shake mine with confidence. She looked like the cover girl from one of those teen magazines with floating text next to her head that reads, "5 Ways to Get Him to Ask You to the Dance!" Yes, she was *that* cute. She sat, we talked, and by the end of class, we were passing notes back and forth making plans for a sleepover.

Our inevitable friendship was always upbeat. She laughed out loud because of me. It truly was my humor that won her heart and the title of "best friend." My ability to make her giggle until she fell asleep earned me rights to more sleepovers. Every night we spent together that summer was invested in lying on the roof to get what we referred to as a "moon tan." We even went so far as to bring up the tanning oil and spray bottles full of water to mist our skin. It was these simple things that made our relationship blissful. But the bliss only lasted until the boys took interest and the bombardment of locker love notes began.

Suddenly, "yours truly" became the jealous gangly friend who didn't understand why her locker was never filled with valentine hopefuls. The boys talked to Sunny as if I did not exist, making the burn worse by rudely mocking my eighties' hairstyle. Of course, her teased, sandy blonde hair was perfect. She must have had the one and only magical can of Aqua Net.

Being her friendly ghost or her attached shadow became my place in the world.

But Sunny never accepted these advances from the boys, and I was confused, was it because she had so many to choose from, or was it something else. After watching Sunny reject many courting fellows, it felt right to explain my feelings using carefully thought out words and expressions. But I didn't prepare for any of it. I just grabbed hold of my sheep print jammies and went for it. There wasn't much thought behind what I said because it came from my heart. My confidence was at a level ten when I said it. I made sure we were alone in case she smacked me to the carpet – 'cuz it could happen. It was during a sleepover while making the bed when my mouth decided that it didn't need to discuss any of what it was about to say with my brain.

"I like you. Like *really* like you." I blurted as I fluffed a pillow and tossed it to the head of the bed. It was a poorly executed statement but boldly done. This was my way of testing her to see what her reaction would be before I went any further. She was on the opposite side of the room gathering more blankets. She immediately said she liked me too but never looked up from what she was doing. Obviously, she didn't catch what I was throwing down, so I said it again with more intention in my voice. "No. I mean, I like you – like you." Then I stood there waiting.

This was me trying to be myself in eighth-grade.

She finally stopped moving and stood up with a dropped jaw. Then she squealed with a high-pitched 13-year-old "Ewe" proceeded by head rolls and hand waves to emphasize her disgust. Neither one of us knew what to do next. We were both embarrassed but for completely different reasons. I didn't say another word as she proceeded to chastise me by calling me a "gay lesbo" who was no longer welcomed to spend the night. Then, when she was done calling me names and saying whatever she wanted to say she attached the last statement like a postscript.

In a total valley-girl accent she said. "By the way, I'll kick your ass if you ever look at me funny again."

I knew I would never mention this to her again nor would I look at her the same. For me, it was done and over in a way, so I let it go. But Sunny wasn't kidding. She didn't want anything to do with a lesbo friend. She blabbed my delicate, unstable claim of passion to my entire eighth-grade class. It traveled through the halls like a lingering fart making everyone scrunch up their noses. This forced me to exploit my sister's new cheerleading popularity to clarify the so-called truth. My sister told everyone that Sunny was a ditz who was completely starved for attention. Four days later, Sunny said she was sorry and invited me to stay the night. This is how kids do things though. We beat each other up on the playground and then boom, best friends. She said she missed our friendship and wanted it back with established limitations. Like the privilege to sleep on the same mattress was gone. My new place in the world was on the floor next to her twin bed. Her stipulation was accepted, and we remained friends just like that. Boom.

After the trauma of saying I liked a girl for the first time, coming out to my parents did not seem super difficult. But the only way to tell them such devastating news was to write a poem. How gay— a coming-out poem. It took me two hours to write. For an eighth grader; this was more than enough time spent on literary arts.

Trying to figure out how to explain myself took months; the whole process of reading my work and trying to say what was clearly said in the poem took minutes.

If only my coming out tale was as elaborate as others. The stories told from gay boys these days are so over the top they must make shit up to earn rainbow colored dick points among their friends.

Every now and then you will hear the truth about how one guy sat his mom down, told her, she cried, and that was it. Those people get an "Aw, that's nice" reaction with a pat on the back. No one buys them an apple martini just for the tale.

People want drama and flair and snapping of the fingers when you tell a coming out story even if it ends in devastation and total family rejection. They want to hear that you cursed out your dad in the garage for calling you a fag when you handed him the flathead instead of the Phillips screwdriver. That you had this deep, emotional, red-faced monologue about drama club or about Carlos, the pool boy. They want to hear about how your mother collapsed in the kitchen and had to be taken to the hospital. How grandma was helping you pack your stuff and found the photos you and Carlos took on the bean bag! They lean on the edge of their seats for it! I tell people that all of the juicy stuff is usually in the middle, then I share my gay-ass coming out – I wrote a fucking poem story.

It took me nearly two hours to write the poem. My stepmother, applying make-up in the burgundy-carpeted master bedroom, provided the perfect opportunity to read it. She was curling her hair, dressed in a bra, skirt, and pantyhose, during my first attempt at coming out. My butt floated on the edge of her water bed as the notepad shook in my hand.

"I wrote a poem, here it goes. You ready?" I waited patiently for her to look my way and give me the accepting head nod which she carefully managed as she held the curling iron in a rolled piece of hair.

"Sure," she said vivaciously to appease my desire for an audience.

I am wondering if I should tell the unsuspecting world of my internal secret

Or if tomorrow is a good place to start.

My eyes broke from the paper to check her reaction. She was motionless as the burning hair spray sizzled from the heat. My hands shook the notepad a bit as the guts and glory of the poem spewed from my lips, but I never looked up from the page then in encore style. I finished:

Or maybe I'll die a meaningless fool knowing I should have told the day before.

In question still.

I waited, poised on the waterbed with bated breath. She rolled another piece of hair around the curling iron and said nothing. There was a long awkward silence, "That's it? Oh, I thought there was more!" She laughed loudly. "Beautiful. Didja write that yourself?" Her heavy Midwestern accent bled into each word and each syllable.

"Yes, it took me two hours. I really poured my heart out." I felt some relief as I gently yet nervously swung my leg back and forth over the edge of the bed.

"It's very good, honey. Yer very talented; you should read that to yer dad." She said.

I kinked the corner of my lips upward in a smile, but I wondered one thing. "Did you get it?"

"Suure," she drew out the word again with her sing-song, Northern Ohio charm that turned the word into a three-note harmony. "Beauta-ful." That was all she said before she teased and puffed her hair higher. My projected heart-to-heart talk with tears and hugs of acceptance never happened. I was left sitting on the waterbed very unimpressed with the way it was handled. I fully expected a dramatic scene like in soap operas complete with orchestral music in the background and close-up shots of our eyes pooling in tears. But this was unexpectedly blasé, and I didn't know what to do with the lackluster moment. It totally threw me off, so I simply jumped off of the bed and shuffled back to my room. After plopping myself on my twin, I began mulling over the months it took to finally tell someone; how it came out in a two-minute poem and how absolutely nothing had changed. My stepmother continued teasing her hair in the other room as I tapped my pencil on the mattress in confusion. She heard my poem but didn't *listen* to what was said.

Later that evening, during a commercial, of course, I read it aloud to my dad. He said he genuinely thought it was well written. When asked if he understood it, he said "yes" just before he un-muted the television to continue watching his show.

My mother's reaction was very understanding. She gave me the "It's-normal-it's-a-phase" speech that every parent in denial feels they are obligated to declare. That's the safe way to say she was a groovy parent, but if I decided to be a raging homosexual in leather ass-less chaps, it better be temporary because she wants grandkids – so don't fuck this up or she will get my demons exorcized! As they say, Mother knows best, so it was written off as a part of growing up.

At this point, rather than focus my energy and new-found sexual tension on the complexities of identity and all that mumbo jumbo, a revolution of porn in the media exposed me to a bigger, more adventurous goal— to touch myself whenever possible because that's what hormonal teenagers do.

Indulging in sneak peeks at my dad's hidden nudie magazines was far more important than the roots of my sexual orientation. My mother's porn collection that she owned with her second husband became one of many sources of entertainment. Forwarding past the man sex to the housewife and Avon lady fucking in the parlor was part of my process. Dear Grandma's romance novels from the bookshelf of her private collection were not safe from the mission to turn myself on. My routine involved flipping to the middle of the book to read about "smooth sun-kissed skin, hard nipples, and hot wet pussy" while Grandma cooked her famous beef and homemade noodles.

She nearly choked on her Pepsi once when she caught me reading one of her cherished Indian and white woman lovemaking scenes. My heart catapulted through my chest when she disrupted my visual of Red Cloud about to give it to his white woman lover in the cabin before her asshole lumberjack husband came back to smack her around.

Jane was arched over the bearskin with her ass in the air feeling intoxicated by the heat of the moment. Red Cloud's bronze skin and animalistic lust for her petite frame made Jane feel every sensation of her throbbing wet mound of passion. Red Cloud couldn't speak English, but he didn't have to say a word to know that Jane's heaving pussy needed to be filled.

The build of tension before Red Cloud inserted his pulsating man beef led the reader into intense anticipation and escalated my body into full masturbation mode. This was when Grandma caught me reading on the floor, and I'm pretty sure it caused me to piss my pants. She took the book and forbade me to read anything else on the bottom two shelves as she explained they were books for adults. She should have let me read about the insertion of Red Cloud's penis into Jane's vagina and how she squirted all over the bearskin before the lumberjack burst through the door with his musket. Damn Grandma for the denial of these adventures.

After Grandma's restriction, my sexual curiosities escalated with no source to draw from. I would have indulged in the entire collection if gone unnoticed. Maybe that's a good thing though. Otherwise, I'd live on a reservation with my husband TuTonka Thunderbird and a papoose on my back. Hey, it could have happened.

Chapter 2

After Grandma caught me with her "adult books," masturbation material derived from other media. From the innocence of words on a page to role-playing in my one-woman show, my imagination became my playground.

My inspiration was characters from science fiction movies. Dungeons and Dragons infiltrated its way into every science fiction movie of the time, so in fantasies, I morphed into a vampire goddess, a fair maiden, or a warrior. Tim Curry played the devil that cut off a unicorn's horn before the world went dark in *Legend*. Tom Cruise's character, the humble peasant boy, tried to save a beautiful maiden from the spell she was under to become a naughty devil bride. There were trolls, a jealous fairy, and treasures to be found. If it was mystical, yours truly used it to fantasize and masturbate at the age of thirteen. These days, young girls just give blow jobs in the band room, but back then it was the intangible that motivated me.

One evening, while feeling particularly randy and unsupervised, I dreamt this scenario where my character was a helpless maiden kidnapped by an evil wizard. Lying immobile on my bed, my brain visualized a wizard hovering over me. He explained his desire for a bride and that I was his chosen one, for dramatic effect I'm sure. But something was missing so to enhance the foreplay I searched intently throughout my closet for a costume. Unfortunately, there was nothing resembling a cool kidnapped bride outfit.

My brain figured the goons who took me had probably tied me up. Every belt and scarf available became part of the fantasy. Excitement about getting seriously kinky overwhelmed me. I placed the accessories on the bed and scurried into the kitchen.

There was a junk drawer with random paperclips, batteries, and plenty of candles. The long white one, for purity, of course, was my object of choice. I washed it several times to kill every possible germ and ran back into my room to tie myself up. Being the hostage of a lovesick wizard – that was the goal. Can you say drama queen?

When I gave myself an intense fantasy filled orgasm for the first time I blushed innocently.

Even with the masturbation adventure under my belt— pun intended— my reputation was as one of the "prude sisters" of junior high school.

My first kiss was to my first love as his dad drove us home from celebrating his sixteenth birthday, a far cry from leather and candles. We kept it simple and sweet by holding hands in the hallway and never giving public displays of affection as he walked me to my classes. Robert carried my books and wrote me love letters. A sideways glance was enough for fulfilling displays of affection. He was a perfect gentleman to me, a good hometown boy. Definitely the marrying type— Robert busted his ass working two jobs to save up for a junkie car and spent more energy on treating me right rather than getting in my pants.

Other than my parents who obviously didn't read into my gay poem and Sunny who told the fucking world, my first love was the person my sexuality was expressed to. It was only mentioned a few times, so we never really had an in-depth conversation according to my faded memory. Robert was far too shy to discuss a topic like that. He couldn't even buy condoms because he stood red-faced and frozen at the end of the aisle and giggled all the way to the car. My virginity would have been lost to him at sixteen had we not used the condoms as water balloons. We jiggled them around for hours. It's a good thing the origin of my sexuality was a boring subject because greasing the prophylactics with shaving cream and trying to pop them with pins was way more fun.

Nevertheless, something unheard of compelled me to look beyond my good old boy. Robert was too perfect. My quote to him was, "I'm too young to be so in love. Maybe we should see other people." He begged me not to and didn't understand why too much happiness with him meant cutting it off. Honestly, it felt like a huge mistake but had to be done because we were so in love it seemed surreal. Many tears were shed when he wasn't waiting for me at my locker anymore.

I tried to date a few other boys after the idiotic dumping of my first love. They were just crushes, temporary interests compared to him. Running back to him seemed the right thing to do, but just like a man, he shagged the first girl that showed interest. Somehow this shocked me as if he should have waited for me as long as necessary. What sixteen-year-old boy would do that?

Escorting oneself through a first heartbreak is never easy.

That is when my mind wandered back to girls. The boys were easy to leave behind when half the girls' volleyball team happened to be in my gym class. Joining the team was a possibility until this tomboy learned that the uniform included "Daisy Duke" spandex shorts. My underwear covered more of my ass than the shorts!

Like a true queen, my extracurricular activities revolved around drama club theatrics. The summer before my senior year I auditioned for a role at my local theater titled *The Secret Garden*, fitting for the tale that follows. A decent role was assigned to me although it wasn't the lead. I was required to be at rehearsals for nearly four days a week. The most desired character was given to the most talented, upbeat girl.

Angel was perfect for the role and had a powerhouse voice to deliver each song she performed. Hearing her sing was never tiresome. For her age, she was very roomy in the hips. The red dress she wore in one of the scenes was this flowing, see-through material, layered enough to blow endlessly in the slightest breeze. During her song, she expressed emotion using hand gestures and swayed her hips to each slow word. The dress, to me, looked like a crackling fire licking gently around her legs. It was mesmerizing. She was a pretty blonde with a hugely welcoming and upbeat personality. I was addicted to her smile, but initially, it was the dress that made me take notice of her body.

The front bodice hung low enough to show the slightest hint of cleavage beneath her first Victoria's Secret bra. When the right light cast as she moved to the edge of the stage, her silhouette glorified the ensemble.

Being turned on by a girl of sixteen singing songs about death makes a person uneasy.

Our friendship grew with each rehearsal, and suddenly, for whatever reason, same-sex relationships came up in conversation. I pried into her sexuality in the wings of the stage and exaggerated about my own flings with women. Angel faked being comfortable as she bashfully explained her inexperience and unwillingness to do it. I reveled in every delicious lie until our names were called for the next scene.

After my admittance of such a taboo subject, things changed between us. The touches became more frequent, never excessive; the laughter became flirtatious rather than friendly. Once, Sprite nearly shot from my nose when she winked at me from across the room. Then one evening during our break from rehearsal, she almost kissed me behind the theatre bushes until a bunch of bastard kids ran past us in the alley, killing the sexual tension.

Caught off-guard I stepped on my own toe while turning to break free from the moment that no one was supposed to see. During my reach for the bushes to cushion my inevitable fall, my hand slid into them, scratching my arm and jabbing a twig into my upper gums. These were my pre-pimp days.

She could barely help me out of the bushes; she was laughing so hard. The stolen moment was forgotten when she pulled me to my feet and asked me to stay the night. There was a strange tingle in my veins as a hot flash crept through me with a sudden burst of unexplainable energy.

It was in her room when the infamous first *real* girl/girl kiss happened. We were seated yoga-style on her bed, facing each other when somehow, in the wee hours of the night, our teenage conversation turned sexual, and we realized our hands had migrated to each other's inner thighs under the blankets. We verbally ignored what was happening and pretended that it wasn't, but our bodies accepted each inching reach until there was an uncomfortable silence as she stared at me in the dark. Our hands bathed in the heat of each other inappropriately close to the cotton lining within our underwear. She was trying to read my facial features for a sign that she wasn't the only one with desires to move forward. "Don't you want to kiss me?" She whispered with undertones of her wishes. Briefly, it felt as if she was in charge and that all of my shit talking about the previous experience was coming to light. My reaction to her question was involuntary.

My sphincter muscle snapped tight right before our kiss actually happened. My body went through the whole gamut of physical reactions including the most amazing twitch I endearingly refer to as the butt-hole pucker.

The butt-hole pucker is the shocking clench of the anus produced involuntarily when encountering unexpected emotions. An array of experiences stimulates this odd malfunction of human anatomy. There is the fear pucker brought on by horror films and death by hang gliding. There is the "Holy crap; I have to shit pucker!" warning its human host of upcoming deposits that desperately need to be made. But the one spoken of accompanies sexual excitement and can be the origin of physical exhilaration. I'm sure that somewhere out there it has been surveyed and documented. Note to self: find butt-hole pucker research. But I digress.

As much as I would like to write about passionate lovemaking in a poetry-perfect world, here are the facts of the clench in my sphincter muscle. When we kissed for the first time after the question was asked, it was the butt-hole pucker that caused me to heave forward, clicking our teeth together. Ah yes, pre-pimp days. Fun. Fun.

After managing to ruin the most important move in a first-time lesbian experience, things began to flow naturally. Transitions from one touch to the other seemed effortless after the initial bumbling idiot phase. We did not make love; we simply gave our bodies to each other and trusted in the moment. Innocence was lost, and freedom found as it ended with passionate kisses before we fell to sleep. We fought our internal battle against traditional Adam and Eve.

Despite the mighty triumph for me, a black cloud of confusion reared its ugly head for her and the next morning Angel did everything she could to avoid eye contact. She made sure there was no physical touch as she sat uncomfortably in a front room chair. Straddling the footstool in front of her was my only opportunity to ask if she was okay. She secretly wanted to smack my hand away and probably felt sick to her stomach, but these were all clues I pulled from her body language.

In my head she wanted me to leave so she could shower and scrub the sin from her body. Visuals of how she gagged herself as she brushed her teeth in the mirror and cried for redemption plagued me. It would be no surprise to me now if someone told me that she was some bible-thumping evangelist because of our unholy "sexcapade," and it was I who turned an angel to temporary insanity and physical lust. Oh, how she would preach to her congregation on the story of Sodom and Gomorrah bearing witness to her testimony of salvation. I would hope that as she fans away the sweat of the Holy Spirit, the pulse in her loins reminds her of the way she licked her fingers free of my cum. In Jesus' name, she prays, Amen.

For her, I was a temptress, the devil incarnate. She was only too relieved when my car drove away from her street to head home. We did not speak until the next afternoon. On my third attempt to call, she finally answered, so my first question was how she was doing. Her response was very abrupt, followed by silence. It's unclear, but she may have been rebuking me at that moment so with a deep breath I switched the handset to my other sweaty palm.

"Look," I said with careful hesitation, "I had a lot of fun yesterday, and maybe we could watch a movie or something tomorrow, you know. I'd really like to see you again." I anxiously twitched and repeatedly rolled the cord in my fingers as my eyes frantically jolted around the room.

Every word fatigued me; the end of the sentences exhausted all of my energy. In the seconds of waiting for an answer, my ears burned while my body became stiff and motionless. My breathing paused, my heart stopped, everything froze. It's a time warp oddity, but that was me, stuck in time, waiting with hot throbbing ears, hoping for an equally deep response to words uttered with huge underlying meaning.

She said my name and sighed deeply with a hint of sad apprehension. It sounded like she almost gave up when she discreetly said she didn't want to hang out with me anymore.

She said 'hang out' to describe what we did, and that was almost as hurtful as the rejection that was about to happen.

Instantly, I knew what she was trying to say and interrupted her in a futile attempt to block her from uttering the words she probably perfected in the shower. "Can I just call you tomorrow?" Immediately I began to sweat.

Her brash answer was no. She was beginning to sound agitated and impatient as if she was constantly scanning her room for unexpected family members. It was obvious the more I talked, the more she wanted the call to end.

I chose my words carefully as I twisted and twisted at the cord until my fingers turned purple at the tips. "But we had such a good time, and I thought…"

"I'm not gay," she said calmly with an attempt to stifle her words from possible prying ears.

My heart burst into a million little pieces. I expected some hostility after she sulked in a guilt trip for twenty-four hours, but I hoped for the Angel who was intimate with me the previous evening. It felt like the person on the phone was the evil twin of a familiar songbird. In reality, she was pushing me away faster than a kid dodges medicine.

In desperation, I begged as if I was only asking a friend for a good day to catch a movie. My voice was timid when I asked. "What about Thursday? Can I call then?"

She snapped at me with her hands over her mouth to the phone which only made the whisper sound very loud. "Don't call me again. I'm *not* gay!" and *click*, hung up the phone. That was it for her— pushed over the edge with Thursday. Maybe the request should have been for Friday or Saturday, that's usually when straight girls go wild. Either way, my mouth stayed open in shock until the receiver beeped. The handset pressed into my hot ear until beeping fell silent to the lost call. Dramatically I spoke to the nothing on the other end, "Okay, I guess I'll call you some other time." Then slowly hung up the phone.

Escorting oneself through a second heartbreak is not easy.

My happiness with undefined sexuality was satisfying until she came along and disrupted everything. She ran from me, so I ran back to men and lost my "true" virginity to a boy I'd barely known longer than a month. It was easier to be straight, and to be honest; boys are far easier to please.

My first love came back into my life through his pregnant girlfriend. She heard through the high school grapevine that we were secretly confessing love while I was dating some idiot in an automotive science class who was, in fact, mildly retarded. Part of it was true; Robert and I talked, but he initiated phone calls and confessed things to me about our love. His words were warm and true. She may have been his girlfriend, but I held his heart.

Hormones must have driven her insane because she confronted me at the top of a set of stairs in school. She stood so close her belly linked the space between us as she threatened to beat me up. My inner butch, needing an excuse to escape, didn't utter a single curse word, but each calculated sentence flew like daggers. Friends were shocked with how eerily calm I was versus my usual vibrancy. When a girl isn't afraid to fight a pregnant woman, it's best to walk away. And she did. There is power in confidence, but no matter how strong you are, someone always wants to test it.

She tested it a second time, weeks later when she drove to my house after a heated phone call. A shouting match ensued just as my parents came home from work. In their infinite wisdom, they thought it best to bring everyone into the house to clear the air in a civilized manner. Of course, my preference was to kick her pregnant lily-white ass.

As everyone seated themselves, my gaze fixated on her sitting beside Robert; I sat crossed legged on the floor, a weakened version of myself. My dad and step-mom were there to mediate our little pow wow.

The bottom line was if Robert said it was over; it was true. Anything else was an obsolete spilling of useless ramblings.

She tried to speak for Robert, but I barked before she could say another word. "You. SHUT. UP. I refuse to hear it from you." My finger pointed between the two of them as her eyes grew to the size of quarters with my unexpected outburst. "I want to hear it from him. I want it to come from HIS mouth; otherwise, it means SHIT to me! Don't you speak for him again!" With quiet defiance, she grabbed his hand and held it in hers. Timidly she spoke, "Tell her Robert. Tell her you don't love her anymore." Her passive-aggressive tactics were pushing my emotional buttons and had my parents not been sitting there, I would have exploded into a rage that wouldn't have ended well.

Robert sat quietly for a moment; he never was much on words. He looked down at their intertwined fingers in contemplation, over to her belly, then to me waiting in a controlled fury on the floor. Everyone fell silent, listening to the beat of their own heart with bated breath as he collected his thoughts. Dad and my stepmom watched the young love drama unfold before their very eyes. Even they were in disbelief at the amount of tension in the living room.

Eventually, he looked me dead in the eye, gently and quietly cleared his throat and said he didn't love me anymore. My parents' devastation added to my own because they truly liked him. They even went so far as to pick him up, put a red bow on him and surprise me for my sixteenth birthday. They knew it would crush me, but they didn't expect it would hurt them too. I could hear their sighs of disappointment as my hands instantly cradled my face in pain and embarrassment. The intent was to bury my tears, but when the flood came, there was no way to hide them. Yours truly cried the most horrific gut-wrenching, heart-breaking cry on the planet. Not because he said the words that destroyed my world but because he was lying.

Deep in the canvas of his soul, he painted a picture of unconditional love for me but hid his work of art for the sake of an unborn child. My pain poured so hard and long that I didn't hear them leave and collapsed an hour later from exhaustion. My dad picked me up from the floor and carried me to my room. He excused me from school as my face was so swollen it affected my vision. I became a zombie of an emotional death, completely lifeless on the inside.

That year the heartbreak from Robert and Angel brought minor isolation issues and rebellion. There was no violence to small animals or other radical mischief; rather fashion was my outlet. My hair was styled in outlandish ways, and Goodwill dresses became my staple for two weeks. Yes, I was a real insurgent trying to rise up against tradition. It's so clever to use fashion as an understatement.

Amber, my best friend, could not be tempted into these ways no matter how convincing my monologue was. Her passive bubbly personality wouldn't allow my rebellion to begin. She accepted me any way presented therefore calming my internal uprising. She was my peacemaker, my confidant. Amber soothed my troubled waters and was a bridge back to normalcy. Recalling her nonchalant reaction after pulling a *Penthouse* from my mattress was relieving and refreshing, and a wonderful surprise considering my struggle and attempts to hide it. Without flinching, she sat down to browse the pages on my bed. She flipped her long blond hair behind her shoulder and opened it exposing the photos inside.

"Why do you have this? This is a guy's magazine."

I was literally in my closet pulling out clothes when she brought it to my attention. By that time, she had already flipped through a few pages. In a panic, I tried to grab it from her hands, but she was too quick. She laughed at my attempt. I was extremely embarrassed but glad to be exposed by my best friend and not anyone else. I stood five feet away with my arms crossed defensively, scared of where this might go, but I explained because there was something accepting in her blue eyes.

"Because I like girls?" I made the statement a question unintentionally showing her how vulnerable I was.

Amber flipped her blonde hair again as she turned another page, never looking up from the naked women in the pictures. "Are you gay?" She asked frankly as she scanned the glossy pages and made a comment about one of the models' beautiful heels.

"I think so. No, I'm bi." I corrected and plopped my ass on the bed next to her. We sat together, skimming its pages and taking note of a few exceptional models that really did something for me. As I pointed to the girls that I liked it dawned on her that I wasn't kidding, and I really had a thing for the same sex.

"Wait, you don't like *me*, do you?" she asked and laughed like she already knew the answer.

"No, you jack ass. You're not my type." I pushed her shoulder unexpectedly and scrunched my face at her as if she disgusted me. Her leg lifted from the floor to balance her weight and prevent a fall off of the bed.

Her eyebrows hit the ceiling as we turned red with laughter. Amber tried to shout through her amusement "That's fucked up!" but she couldn't quite catch her breath and choked on her spit. That only sent us into a hysterical giggling fit. When she finally got control of herself after coughing into her fist, she genuinely said, "I don't care what you are, you're just Janell to me." She was sincere; she was direct and held eye contact with me as she said it to let me know that whoever I turned out to be; she was supportive.

That being established, her curiosity reared its head, and she asked if I had ever physically been with a girl.

That's when my confession of Angel and the details of our night together occurred for the first time, including the phone call the next day. When my eyes became misty, I diverted her attention to a story about a girl in our class who was also our mutual friend. Amber was jealous of this girl, so when her name was mentioned, she listened intently.

The girl's best friend recently confessed years of love for her, so she was considering a lesbian relationship. The juicy part was that I was interested and wanted to be more than friends. It was shocking, but Amber was so fascinated by the drama she didn't care about the dynamics of being gay or bisexual. It was the sensational details she wanted to know more about. I indulged her with answers to any questions that followed, none of which ever became an issue again.

Once Amber knew about Robert and Angel's rejection, and the love triangle, she completely understood why it was important to get the hell out of Ohio. She knew the quickest way out was to join the military.

Chapter 3

It was difficult holding back my sexuality after coming to realize who I was. It's like trying to announce the cure for cancer in a whisper. Typically, when gay people come out of the closet, they become flamboyant with their newly discovered, or accepted identity. Some own all the rainbow trinkets and make it obvious that they fought to be themselves. It's a rite of passage in the community.

My inner confidence was gained by owning the title of true bisexual. I use the word "true" to establish credibility for the label. It sets apart the stereotypical girls in college who finger their best friends on a drunken horny rampage from the bisexuals who struggle early on. Inner confidence, however, did not earn me sexual freedom. Inhibiting myself was essential to enter the realm of don't ask, don't tell, so I could be all I could be. Definitely, some irony to be noted here.

In basic training there was a very good-looking girl bathing directly across from me in the community showers, claiming to hate gays. "Olive Oil," dubbed so by the drill sergeants for her thin frame and slicked black hair. She was just the girl next door until the bubble thong incident. She became my living entertainment after she doubled up in a shower, giggling loudly not to worry, she was straight. Immediately my eyes scanned the area, scouting for the girl who made the comment. I would never have looked twice until she unknowingly challenged me with those words.

After that, my gaze intentionally lingered over her smooth perfection as my way to counterbalance her hatred for that which she claimed to know. Olive babbled about how she would *know* if a girl in the bay was a lesbian. On and on she spewed as she scrubbed the shampoo through her hair, causing her perfect size C's to bounce in rhythm.

While "listening," I wondered what she would do if she knew I was lustfully looking at her body. A giggle pulled me out of my trance in just enough time to hear her say *I'd kick her ass* before she trailed off again into *blah blah blahs*. My smile was timed with everyone else's, but secretly she transitioned into my personal porn.

The shampoo slid down her sun-kissed curves. It began at the nape of her neck, over her shoulders, and through the center of her chest. It split into two foamy lines at her navel. One fell straight through her pubic hair; the other followed the contours of her hips to the back. I stared too long and became red-faced with embarrassment, but no one was watching me to notice my reaction. The girls were far too enthralled in Olive's story on being anti-gay to see just how simply erotic she looked in that bubble belt. When she turned to wipe the soap from her eyes, the shampoo followed her spine directly through the crack of her perfect eighteen-year-old ass.

The bubble thong incident let my inner confidence on bisexuality grow into that cure for cancer whisper. A rainbow began to appear over my heart, but there were no pride parades for me that year.

After boot camp, I trained to learn the job I would eventually perform in the military. At that point, my sexuality was set in bisexual stone. However, my attention gravitated toward the only known lesbian within the first three days of being at the school. My bisexual proclamation was mentioned freely so the "rumor" would get to her.

This passive-aggressive way to show interest was worse than sending a message by carrier pigeon. Only God knows if she heard any of it at all. If she did, she was absolutely one hundred percent indifferent. She was blinded by lust and doted over her roommate aka "lover." She remained infatuated and called it love.

My first time meeting her was after overhearing girls chatter in the hall. Initially, my intent was to shut them up, but the lesbian was sitting, crying in the doorway of a room with five nosey girls surrounding her. Anyone with a curiosity bone would have investigated the scene as quickly as I did. The snot was oozing from her nose, but she was too upset to care and never bothered to wipe it away. Slurs through her beer breath had all of us standing close enough to comfort her, yet far enough to inhale fresh air.

Between sobs, the lesbian managed, "I mean why? That bitch, I did everything for her. Gave her anything she wanted!"

Her head fell back in desperation or exhaustion and hit the door jamb. She didn't seem to care about this either. With a sudden burst of anger, she yelled, "Fucking dick! She went for a dick!"

The six of us listened to the obvious pain she was going through. A few paid attention with curiosity rather than compassion until she mumbled, "I love her." Then they tilted their heads to the side and swooned as if they really understood. She cried with her head between her knees as we all hovered without a shred of advice to give.

Rachel, a short black-haired beauty, was the first to say anything at all and the first to help this girl to her feet. She spoke with a smooth even tone as she looked to me, silently asking for a hand in guiding the lesbian down the hall. My place at that moment was under the arm of the broken-hearted as we carried the lesbian and the weight of her burden successfully to her room.

We asked if there was anything she wanted before turning out the light. She never said a word. The lesbian walked to her bed, sat for a second, walked to the other bed, and lay in the scent of her lover's empty sheets. We shut the door on her torment and exhaled in relief.

This is too intense for me. I need a smoke," I said as I tucked my hair behind my ears and turned to walk away.

To my surprise, Rachel followed me to the doorway of my room down the hall. She was excited to accompany me on a forbidden smoke break in the wood line where someone had cleared an area and created seating out of fallen trees. After we grabbed our coats, we walked to it in the dark, stopping at the edge where a street lamp burned bright to light our cigarettes before pushing on into the trees where the glow didn't reach. We walked onward to the strategically placed clearing as we talked about simple things like how she loved smoking in the dark because she enjoyed seeing the fire burn brighter when she inhaled. Her contrasting black hair over pale white skin captivated me as we discussed the lesbians' issues and my bisexuality. She listened intently with widespread brown eyes as I explained my first love's and Angel's rejection.

It was awkward to recognize my growing attraction to Rachel, but she was comfortable with flirtation. Before my finished cigarette became the reason to end our conversation another one miraculously appeared between my lips while her head was turned. I patted every pocket searching for the lighter that must have fallen out through a hole.

Rather than hand me her lighter, Rachel held it to my smoke with the flame ready. She lit my cigarette in the dim getaway while possessing me with her sparkling chocolate eyes. The night chill took over our bodies. We joked how each drag of the cigarette temporarily stopped our shivering. We giggled and shook as the air grew colder.

Because I became comfortable, I was compelled to tell Rachel of my interest in her. She listened to my compliments without flinching or disgust. She was patient and non-judgemental as I expressed my admiration. Her smile simply broadened before she clarified her preference for men with a coy head turn to the side that was somewhat contradicting.

I didn't feel ashamed or embarrassed or even rejected. I felt accomplishment for my first real expression of interested in someone of the same sex. Then I became a little cocky. "Well, that's a shame. You are too pretty and sexy to reserve yourself for a man," I said assuming that would be the end of it. I wanted to leave her something to think about later.

But she threw me for a loop and stared me down with conviction. "I've wondered," She inhaled a long drag from her smoke as she peered into my eyes. The crickets and mosquitos were few as the temperatures began to drop with seasonal changes. The bitter wind rushed through what was left of the leaves that seemed to hush the moment into an unexplainable stillness. Returning her glare, the best I could through the darkness, sparks of hope burst in my heart and crotch. I leaned into her next words as the wind pushed my hair into my face. "But I try to lead a Christian life and just wouldn't do something like that." I pulled my upper body away from hers as the smoke billowed from her mouth with each word. It shut my excitement down like a switch.

She cocked her lips sideways and blew out the last bit from her lungs before inhaling fresh, crisp air again. What a vixen.

Each move she made reminded me of the legendary pin-up, Bettie Paige, a woman taboo for her time because of her attitude on sex. Not only did Rachel look like her but shared a similar faith in Jesus Christ our Savior. Not many people know about Bettie's strong foundation in the church because of her overshadowing modeling career. To be honest, most don't even know that she began as a legitimate fashion model.

Average Americans know Bettie Paige from kinky leather clad photo shoots where she was depicted spanking other girls with catlike prowess. Her perceived sexuality came from within as she smiled and had fun with her portrayal of a dominatrix. Her swimsuit modeling career was dominated by the risqué photos she posed for in the days when men could get arrested for buying filth like that. The taboo photo opportunities were short-lived, but no one seems to remember the beginning of her career or how she tried to go back to acceptable modeling after it.

Bettie actually ended her modeling career to be a preacher of the word of God. She claimed the photos simulating sadomasochistic acts were lighthearted and never understood why it was wrong if she was covered with clothing. After all, Adam and Eve were nude in the Garden of Eden, and no one had dammed and judged them but God himself.

Everything about Rachel reminded me of Miss Bettie in those old pinup calendars. Rachel had the same bubbly smile and a whimsical sense of humor with an undeniable sexuality just like Bettie Paige. She was a vixen with a cross around her neck, a twisted, beautiful mess of good versus evil. It made her more alluring yet more unobtainable at the same time. After Rachel explained how she was set in her religious beliefs and wouldn't be with a woman, she reached out to gently touch my face. The smell of her peach hand lotion hit me, and I was surprised I hadn't smelled it before then. Her touch was soft as she stroked my cheek with the back of her bent fingers. It seemed as if she was lingering in contemplation, "Thanks anyway. You are beautiful." She dismissed me verbally but added a wink.

It is the teasing nature of Bettie Paige's pictures that made her famous, but that was also the crap Rachel used to manipulate me with. It was like man versus dog. She is the owner teasing me, the dog, with a toy until there is a pool of drool at my paws. She squeaks the toy excitedly and gives it a long throw commanding me to fetch, at which I obediently run, sniff, and twirl around the area. Meanwhile, there is Rachel coaxing me to find the toy when it is still in her hand behind her back. She laughs at how cute it is to watch me sniffing for a toy she never let go. The wink and the compliment was Rachel teasing and laughing at her lovable dumb dog for falling into such an obvious trick.

Rachel puffed on her smoke with a glorious smile and a strange, confident ease after complimenting me. Her black hair fluttered across her white moonlit cheek. That wonderful moment will always be captured in my mind.

She seemed so unfazed by my attraction to her yet welcomed my advances with what felt like advances of her own. It felt right to shoot her a smooth, silent head shake and the most perfect wink and smile combination. James Dean himself couldn't have done it better. The actor would have been proud of my single-handed flick of the cigarette into the darkness. Shit, all I needed was a leather jacket, another cigarette in my mouth, a tree to lean against with one leg up, and she would have been at my feet, begging me to change her mind. It was legendary.

Replacing being gay with confident assurance in bisexuality worked for me around the time of Rachel and the lesbian. They didn't want me, and I didn't fit their established roles. I was attracted to guys, the boyish ones with hairless faces and big eyes. I liked the flirtation and ran with it, becoming promiscuous. It was fun to have so much power as a woman in a man's world. Girls were attractive but not as sexy as Rachel, straight or otherwise. Every opportunity to make her blush was taken then retracted only when it seemed to make her uncomfortable. After a while, it became expected of me to flirt. We both understood it was genuine yet subdued out of respect.

It started during our smoke breaks, and eventually, smoking became our tradition, our common ground and excuse to bat eyes at each other. While I endlessly patted my pockets down for a lighter that always seemed to be missing, we spent the time talking about various things.

Eventually, the months grew colder, and even with jackets, it was too frigid to stand around for an hour enjoying our cigarettes. We stopped our rendezvous all together until one day she pulled me into the bathroom stall as I headed to my room. She must have been watching for me because it was perfectly timed.

As I stumbled into the common bathroom with laughter she whispered in excitement, "Come smoke with me; look there is a vent in this one," pointing to the top of the wall in the far stall. It took her beautiful brown eyes a few flutters with a bit of begging before I agreed. We giggled as we squished into the stall, lit our cigarettes, and tried to blow our exhales into the slats as quickly as we could so we wouldn't get caught.

Suddenly someone flushed a toilet and fear drained the color from both of our faces. The sound echoed through the stalls and tiled walls. In a panic, we rid ourselves of the evidence and walked out to the sinks as if two girls coming out of a stall was normal. The lesbian was there, squishing soap in her hands with a smile from ear to ear while she remarked, "Don't worry ladies, that's where I go," and nonchalantly rinsed.

This time we were safe from the wrath of the drill sergeants, but we cleared ourselves from the latrine just the same. We understood with words unspoken that this was our new designated smoking area and the routine resumed in the warmth of the stall. It was also my overdue fix to see Rachel, but it ended too quickly. So off I went to have sex in the woods with an equestrian boy from Ohio.

It took about a week before Rachel, and I stopped blowing the smoke into the slats figuring it didn't make a difference as long as the girls continued to bitch about the odor.

Since no one could be pinpointed as the culprit, all the smokers became careless. What would "they" do anyway? Kick us out of the Army for smoking? We laughed at our rebellious actions. Rachel was the minx who brought up that fact.

Our routine made me happy, but it also led me to my most uncomfortable situation with Rachel. The smoking tradition was as follows; we met, checked the latrine, smoked and talked, washed our hands, and left. It was perfectly timed to coincide with the absence of other soldiers and drill sergeants. No one ever came in, and if they did, we were too wrapped up in the moment to notice. On one such smoke break, I lost control and had hope of something more.

As the story goes, we met, as usual, checking the latrine stalls for feet and opening the shower curtains just in case. We prepped the vent for the proper angle, and I took my usual position against the back wall, straddling the toilet while she pulled out a cigarette for each of us and leaned against the door. It was the routine and the details of it that made the whole ordeal more than just a smoke break. I patted down every pocket possible for the lighter that I swore was on me this time. Rachel snickered at my familiar actions and shook her head as she held two cigarettes in one hand and crossed her arm over her stomach with the other.

"Wait, dammit, I know I put one in my pocket today." I patted myself down relentlessly as she watched endearingly with her big brown eyes.

"Yeah, like you put one in your pocket yesterday and the day before, right?" Her head shook again, but this time it was accompanied by deep eye rolls.

"Shut up, you ass. Where the hell do they go? I must have a fucking hole in my pants." I countered and continued checking the ten possible pockets in my uniform. We snickered in unison as I checked for the third time.

While I mumbled on about a lighter that was never there, she slipped her hand into her pocket and pulled from it a pink mini Bic. Rachel placed her hand on my shoulder to stop me, and when I looked up from the hunt, she placed a smoke into my mouth and reminded me, "Here, I have mine." Her peach hand cream was recently renewed, and the smell was stronger than usual. But I was fixated on locating the missing one which was supposed to be in on me. Was it because I was trying to prove my point or that I was avoiding eye contact?

Either way, I was losing cool points the longer I fumbled. "I swear I have it. I grabbed it to impress your dumb ass and used it to burn strings from the lesbian's uniform in formation."

Rachel formed a half-cocked smile, and her eyes changed. I couldn't see the change; it wasn't something visual; I could only *feel* it. My boots scooted back an inch for spatial comfort. My tone changed in frustration but held flirtatious undertones. "God damn it, woman, stop smirking. I know it's here." It was a lighthearted stubbornness. Rachel plastered the Mona Lisa smile across her lips as she stared at me much longer than she ever had. This stare confirmed the difference in the atmosphere. My embarrassment was quite obvious.

"What?" I asked as she stared and said nothing.

My hands nervously squeezed each pocket. The filter on the cigarette in my mouth was getting wet with each passing second. The fan next to the vent stopped spinning. Her glare made me incredibly uneasy so bending over a bit to "check" my cargo pockets for the fourth time was the best way to hide the blushing that was filling my cheeks. The tension seemed to make the stall enclose around us.

Her words replayed over in my head about how she was totally Christian, which only made me feel guilty about the signals she was presumably sending. As I leaned down, Rachel shifted her position from the stall door. She sidestepped and moved closer to me with her lighter already in flames yet gave me enough room to straighten myself up.

"I told you I have mine." She waved the lighter in the air. As the smell of peach and burning lighter fluid filled my nose our eyes locked; then she stole another inch of my space. The bright flame created a beautiful reflected flickering in her eyes, and I was mesmerized. I could almost see my frozen image staring back at me.

Rachel held the lighter and as I uncomfortably broke my stare with a shake of my head. My eyes focused on the tip of the cigarette to make sure it was in the flame. As I inhaled, our eyes reconnected through the haze and yours truly was unable to feel confident about anything. I'm sure my eyebrow shifted to silently ask her what she was doing. I was perplexed and extremely coy which is highly unlike me and only convinced her of the power she had. She nudged her body against mine, barely, but it was enough to make my knees feel weak and start the ringing in my ears.

    I tilted my head back when the cigarette was lit and exhaled the smoke into the air as our bodies hovered close enough to bathe in each others' radiating heat. "Thank you," I said in the way that smokers do when they still have it in their lungs and need to take another breath.

    My gaze flicked back to her, and alarm shot through me. She had managed to lean her face closer to mine while distancing the physical connection between our bodies. There was a pause and the fantasy of us kissing that overwhelmed me.

    I restrained everything my body was telling me to do and let confusion rule my actions.

    My observations shifted to her lips and back to her eyes again. She was on the verge of saying something, but I couldn't tell what. We lingered in the moment. Rachel's expression communicated loud and clear that she wanted me, but wanted me to what? Kiss her? Fuck her? Try something so she could call me evil and restate her firm beliefs in Christianity?

    Disconnecting myself was easy. I just inhaled more smoke. My knees finally bent to enable me to sit on the toilet. Rachel smiled. We didn't say much as we finished what was left of our cigarettes. We walked out of the stall, sliding past each other in an aching, desperate state. For once this dog didn't run to the toy that was clearly in the master's hands.

A few days later Rachel invited me to her room unexpectedly during an average conversation before formation. She pulled me off to the side so others wouldn't hear and in a hushed voice asked me to spend the night with her.

"My roommate left for her duty station. Do you want to have a sleepover tomorrow? It's the weekend, and the drills don't come around for bed check." She didn't take a breath until she was finished.

In using the phrase "sleepover" Rachel unknowingly turned anything sexually implied into something totally innocent for me. My brain converted all conversation thereafter into the mundane because she pushed her strong convictions of faith regardless of the bathroom incident and what I thought it meant. I'm sure the flame of hope was still burning dimly somewhere; I just chose not to see it anymore.

Midafternoon the next day we played a card game called Go Fish in her room. Fitting it seemed for the game she was playing with me. It had been a yo-yo of yes and no signals since the day we walked to the wood line to smoke after the lesbian fell to sleep. Her faux advances were entertaining and enjoyable until it was one time too many. The whole bathroom incident was bold, and frankly, it scared me. She had brainwashed me into a set of boundaries, and when she crossed them to indulge herself in being an overt tease, I shut myself off from her.

How rude was it to dangle affections in front of my face and pull them away during my hesitant reach for them? My passions and secret desires for girls were in infancy stages then. My protection against women like her had not been built yet. She was playing games as a trained guard dog, far too advanced for me to ever catch up. I tucked my tail in submission as she barked her dominance. I already cowered and pissed myself in her presence, what more did she want?

This is what happened with our flirtatious easygoing non-sexual, sexual relationship. Rachel became the mean trophy winning Doberman while I remained a whelping puppy running back to its bitch. It was the teasing fetch game in a different dynamic, and I fell for it… again.

She didn't receive my "friend" signal to show that I'm not interested in "that way" even though that afternoon was intentionally turned into childlike playtime. What a better way to be unsexy than to drink can after can of Coke and relish in small victories through burping contests? We played cards, listened to music, and I left as if everything was just peachy. However, returning later for the sleepover, my mouth was full of cotton, and my palms were coated with sweat.

I would have taken friendship over being a pawn in another game, but I wanted her more than a friend. There was no way to hide it. When she answered the door, she took an immediate step into the hallway and pushed me into it. There was a preformed apology in her eyes. My nervous smile went limp, and my eyebrows scrunched together in confusion as I stepped back to catch my balance.

She had already slipped into a t-shirt pajama top; I noticed her nipples poking at the material just before she crossed her arms and looked at me with extreme worry. "I'm sorry. After you left, I went to chow, and when I came back, there was a girl sleeping in my bunk. I have a roommate now so you can't spend the night." She subconsciously ran her fingers through her short hair to make sure each section was in its proper place.

"Why not, will she tell the drills?" I asked as I followed suit and crossed my arms

Rachel shrugged in disappointment. "You can still stay with me if you want. I'm just sad because I thought we would get to be alone." Again, she fidgeted with her hair as if she was primping without a mirror.

Ladies and gentlemen, to this day even when I write the words that came out of her mouth I hear, *"Fetch and get the toy! Good girl."* But in the moment, it blew over my head as the word "straight" appeared like a pop-up label over the top of her head.

"It's no big deal; we're not doing anything bad." My face crinkled with conviction as I uncrossed my arms and placed each hand over her shoulders. "I'm staying." I opened her door and theatrically displayed the entrance to her room with my hands as if to say ladies first. She mumbled several phrases of disappointment before she accepted the situation and stepped inside.

The new girl was asleep in the top bunk when Rachel shook her awake to explain our arrangement. The poor girl grumbled and rolled over, mumbling something about getting caught by the drill sergeants. We ignored her and crawled into the bottom bunk. Rachel slid into the blankets next to me. We tried desperately to whisper so the new girl wouldn't be able to make out one word. Conversation was nearly inaudible at times unless we aimed our words carefully.

I lay face up, constantly scooting closer to the wall. Each time I asked Rachel if she had enough room, she would shift to tell me yes and somehow gain a few inches to my dead pose. She was on her left side and had nuzzled her face to fit on my pillow. I remained composed even though her breath was tickling the hairs on my neck and the sound of each exhale was making me wet. She asked simple questions in my ears making them ring in excitement. My head felt light, but my body was stiff as a board with arms protectively crossed over my stomach. In a lighthearted teasing moment, she deemed me a vampire and nervously giggled before a long silence.

When she again asked if I was settled, it was only her ploy to lead in subtly before a much deeper question. "Why don't you scoot closer to me?" Her whisper made my skin jump.

Here's your toy. (Squeak) Who wants their toy? (Squeak).

My dumb ass response: "No I'm good. I always sleep like this." Another long pause.

"Can I scoot closer to you?" The goosebumps pushed outward, and I began wiggling my big toe as a way to nervously release the tension.

Fetch. Go get it, girl!

The only thing I could possibly say to turn this into something more innocent was, "Why? Do you not have enough room?" As we whispered our flirtations, I made desperate attempts to turn what she was saying into something legitimately unisexual, but she was pushing every button on my control panel.

She moved closer to me and exhaled.

"It's okay; you can touch me if you want." She held her breath and to be honest, I believe she was as stunned to say it as I was to hear it. Then we fell silent before the beat of my chest blasted through my body like a jackhammer.

I didn't do a fucking thing. This was the fake throw for sure. Instead of running to retrieve vacant hope, I lay unflinching. It was the beginning of taking control and understanding the exchange that was happening between us. Have you ever seen a dog smile?

Rachel looked at me through the dark waiting for anything to happen, for me to fetch the toy as she held up empty hands because she threw it and really meant it; no tricks.

But the boy who cried wolf too many times was eaten in the end because nobody came.

And that is exactly how I felt. Somehow this thought gave me the rush of adrenaline I needed to confidently tell her that too many tricks on my people means that nobody comes. In the most delicate yet stern manner, I leaned into her ear and cracked the syllables in each word. "Your roommate is *right* above us."

My enunciation was perfect with an additional pop on the *t* when pronouncing "right." This was very intentional to make it feel orgasmic.

Then I panicked.

My confidence diminished when she assured me the girl above us was sleeping. Fuck I couldn't win with her because again, she was dead serious. Was this a new game? As her chew toy for months, my first reaction was that she was crying wolf again, only in another language.

Then any doubts about her intentions clearly ended when she said, "I want you to touch me, it's ok." yet I lay with her, unable to move. The torment of rushing chemistry burned my skin. She will never know how she reduced me to a pathetic mass of flesh stupefied by her forwardness. I remained motionless as she took each breath near my ear in anticipation. We fell to sleep in this position waiting for the other to make the first move.

The flirting ended after the sleepover as did the smoke breaks. We didn't talk anymore, and before the week was up, Rachel left for her first duty station. I searched for her at the bus stop where all the newly trained soldiers stood waiting to begin their journey into an exciting life of being all that they could possibly be. A recruit next to me read the name on my uniform and asked, "Hey, you're Janell?"

"That's me," I replied.

"I have a message for you from Rachel; she left a half hour ago. She says goodbye and that you had your chance, whatever that means."

My jaw dropped, and my eyes widened with that universal surprised look. I didn't know what to say or think, so I just turned and quickly headed back to the barracks as I mumbled to myself.

"What a twat! Are you kidding?"

It was the final "ta-da!" for Rachel to send me such a message after the behavior she demonstrated over the months. The salt in the cut of the finger, if you will, the wind resistant candle on the fucking cake. It shouldn't have felt like such a shock for her to tease me beyond the last moments of her stay. You just know she was on the bus smirking at her vixen reflection as she shifted in her seat. My immediate reaction was to tell the lesbian the final dig of the she-devil. Her last comforting quote to me was, "That's fucked up, but you're not even gay so don't worry about it."

Rachel never became my third heartbreak. She did, however, earn her medal of "Best in Show" for her dog-like behavior, a crowd favorite in the final lineup. She was the most agile, quick-witted, cunning, beautiful bitch I ever saw. If anything, the Pavlov dogs and I go way back because of Rachel. She had me conditioned to salivate at the wink of her eye. She was *my* bell to stimulate arousal rather than hunger. My body reacted in the same fashion every time she looked at me. Unlike the Pavlov dogs, I didn't get my treat after each ring. When she rang, I became hungry for her, and she neglected me. This is cruelty at its finest. I'm turning her in. The ASPCA should get my letter with her name on it in seven to ten days.

Unashamed

Chapter 4

Poetically speaking, the rainbow colors on my heart faded as military bearing played a role in the person I was becoming. From the bubble thong incident to Rachel, my identity became more defined, but my responsibility was to perform my duties over any struggle with sexual orientation.

At eighteen I had to portray myself as a respectable soldier, but let's be honest, deep down I was a lost Midwestern girl and on my own for the first time in Arizona after my job training. There was a false sense of liberation being so far away from home. Sure, there was money in my savings account and a new car, but my interest was in doing what I wanted, when I wanted, *if* I wanted. It was all about me.

The whole gay thing flew out the window for a time when the discovery of legal drinking for under 21 was allowed on post. My mission in life was to dance until my heart exploded every weekend. Club Ozone was a utopia considering the only bar I had known was a shack surrounded by corn fields, downwind from a pig farm. The Ozone was newly built and frequented by single soldiers and new recruits still learning their future military occupations. It was like a controlled spring break every weekend. There was drinking and dancing and sex and barfing until the hangovers came every Sunday.

Young soldiers knew the drill as did the seasoned ones, who had to endure the aftermath of alcohol coming out of their pores on Monday morning runs. Hell, they did it too back when their livers could withstand the abuse. It's part of an unwritten initiation process of a buck private.

In my early days of partying, I never let myself get intoxicated to the point of wearing it as a perfume the next morning. It was, however, my excuse to sleep around. Women were not a part of my promiscuity, but a few close friends knew that I was *that way*.

Annica, my roommate at my first duty station, was one of the first military friends I came out to. She was open and very frank; of course, it could have been how fast she spoke. By the time she knew what she was saying, it was already eight paragraphs later. She was a hyper girl with glasses and had a slight stutter to make it worse. We used to joke that I was the only one who understood what the hell she was actually saying other than her momma and God. She was bold too. It was typical during a tirade about cooking meat properly to suddenly hear some unexpected shit that made your head spin.

"Blah blah, check it for blood, blah blah temperature should be blah blah, barbeque sauce blah blah, like a dick on your face blah blah, if you are into incest and that sort of thing."

What? Wait. What the fuck?

"I'm just saying the f-fuckin' place up the street didn't cook my steak right and it'll be a cold d-day in hell when the cows jump over the fuckin' moon before I go b-back there again."

During one of her infamous rants she blurted, "You like girls, don't you?" in such a matter of fact way that arguing or hiding the fact was pointless. The shocking boldness of it required the truth. Her evidence to the claim was that of the many images of the singer, Tori Amos; I hung the posters that were most provocative and that straight girls typically did not paint sexy figures of women and hang them.

Annica pushed the bridge of her glasses to the back of her face, "My friend came over here yesterday and thought I had a male roommate. He said that he t-thought the photos of you were my roommate's girlfriend. I just told him you liked Tori Amos when he asked if you were gay. I don't want to t-throw your business out there... I got you, girl."

Rather than take a breath after the sputter of words, Annica took a drag from her cigarette. She was a chain smoker; the ones who smack the alarm and knock the damn thing over trying to feel for her pack and lighter. Observing this every hangover Sunday was my morning ritual. She would open her eyes only after the cigarette was placed in her mouth and she needed to light it. She never sat up until it was down to the filter and burning her fingers. Then maybe she would adorn herself with glasses so she could see.

After she protected my secret all that could be said was thanks while analyzing my clothes, posters, and displayed pictures. What about those things gave the impression I was a man or gay for that matter? There had to be other girls who owned photos of themselves and friends randomly pinned to cheap message cork boards, other girls who liked female singers and taped them to their walls and lockers. I had a photo of Angel and me in our Secret Garden costumes making silly faces, my arm around her shoulder but how is that gay?

When Annie was at work, I removed the gay posters and my drawing of a female silhouette embedded within a pair of red lips. It was terrible anyway. I peeled a magazine page that read, "Men are from Mars, Women are from Mars. Any questions?" off the wall above my desk. Was that gay?

My hand brushed the dust from the frame with Angel, and I immortalized in that happy moment before gently placing it in the desk drawer, face down. Next was de-gaying the cut photos on the cork board that were taped and push-pinned to fit.

After scanning each picture, replaying the moment it was taken in my head, I began to see with new eyes. Each photo was of me with friends, female friends. They wore makeup, had long hair and were usually giving me a kiss on the cheek. There was the occasional boob grab accompanied by a ghetto fabulous pose and/or someone giving the universal sign for lesbian with the tongue between two fingers. This was the kind of immature thing any girl of eighteen does when they have a girl's night out. How does this normal act make me appear gay?

I stood and analyzed the photos for quite some time, before peering over to the drawer that wasn't quite closed. The back of the frame to the overturned photo haunted me. I could almost hear a voice coming from the darkness which repeated "Lesbian" over and over and over.

Looking deeper, the tomboy with little makeup and short hair was me. There was an uncut centrally placed photo that dominated the board. In it, I was seated on my plaid chair, leaning forward wide legged, with my elbows on my knees and a bottle of some alcoholic beverage dangling in my fingers. No posing, just me in my favorite chair waiting for my friend Lynn to get ready for the club.

She was the friend in the photos always pretending to lick her fingers and touch her nipples, the one doing the infamous tongue through the peace sign at the camera. She was the one who snapped the photo of me and Annica after she told us to do the same. Lynn was the one who told me how good I looked in that central picture; I counteracted the compliment by saying it must be the chair. Is that gay?

I was wearing a brown button-down shirt with a pair of jeans and my 1930s newsboy hat, smartly purchased at the thrift store. Bringing back old styles was trendy. My makeup was overdone with dark colors, lipstick, and glitter via a suggestion from Lynn. A cross necklace dangled from my neck. My smile was big and happy. This photo of me was perfect. It just looked like me, very comfortable, and that's why it was celebrated in the middle. With my new eyes, there was an unfeminine tomboy beneath the makeup, sitting in that chair. This was very different from Lynn, who had long curly hair and never went a day without lipstick or jewelry. My look was boyish even under the face paint— or was it dyke-ish?

I began to question the presentation of myself. Did I want people to notice subconsciously or was there serious ignorance to how I portrayed myself? The query hit deep just like the pushpins used to poke through each of my red eyes. This anonymous friend who judged me didn't know me but saw all too well.

Annica understood where my comfort zone was with regard to my sexuality having pieced it together over months. She accepted and never judged me even when I slept with a different guy every weekend. On several occasions, she consoled me as I wept about hating myself. She smoked through her counsel, which made me feel as if my actions were a normal part of finding myself. She made it okay to feel confused and understood my struggle. It was always hangover Sundays after she had put out her morning smoke and picked up the alarm clock from the floor, when I needed the pep talk from her. My tears would be fresh, hot, and somewhat cut with alcohol as I sat on the edge of my bed ashamed "I did it again, Annie."

She never gave me the privilege of a morning greeting when Sunday confessions warranted consultation. She skipped that unnecessary pleasantry to "tisk me." The only time Annica didn't blurt out something without taking a breath was when she hummed "mmm hmmm" in agreement with my Sunday declaration of guilt. It was usually accompanied with a shake of her head and a puckered mouth. This particular Sunday was no different.

"Why do I do this to myself, Annie? I don't even like doing it. I'm such a slut." Snot fell from my nose and began to dribble on my upper lip before I wiped it with my sheets to reiterate another empty proclamation against being the barracks hoe. "Next weekend Annie I'm not bringing anyone home. Fuck that. I'm going to go out and have a good time with you and the girls, and I'm coming back alone. And if you see me getting crazy and trying to do the dirty with some asshole, you stop me okay, Annie?" She tisked me before we agreed on a pact that would secure my new attitude against men, which got me excited about going out again. That was usually the reason to consider it at all.

So, after coming home and frantically pulling my boots off, I'd begin my ritual in preparation for the infamous girl's night out. I'd eat a little something, clean my room, shit, shower, shave, and lay out clothes for the club; that was my routine. The music played loud as we painted our faces, traded jewelry, and shaped our hair to look just right.

As we walked down the hall, all of the other horny young soldiers doing the same thing made the atmosphere comfortable. Each inhale in the hall was the scent of starch from the guys pressing their shirts, aftershave that was overused, women's watermelon body spritz, and burning hair spray. The doors were usually left ajar so walking by each room was like changing the station on your radio. A different song spilled loudly from behind the wooden doors making it a tragic situation for the soldier who just wanted to catch up on sleep.

The building was alive and pulsating until nine thirty when everyone gathered into their groups of five or more and headed out with one poor sap as the designated driver. Then it was as if there was an outbreak of scabies and an evacuation had taken place. Every swinging dick was off the premises, miles from militant control. Stillness befell the hallway, broken by that one random song from the person who hadn't made plans in time and was left to sulk in their room. The lingering stench of weekend party preparations hung low and melted into one unidentifiable yet strangely familiar smell. This was life, every weekend for the first year of my military career.

The Ozone was huge and clean and full of new recruits to choose from. It was really up to me to decide who I wanted because they were all pawns. Every guy whether interested or not was very willing to sleep with me. Each one bought me drinks and left me alone if I told them to because they were trained that no means no by the military's zero tolerance for sexual harassment rules. The club was at my control. I called the shots and manipulated the pawns in my favor. There was serious humor in buddies' cock-blocking each other to gain my attention. But they stuck together like true soldiers should.

There was always a wingman to whisk away any girlfriend warning me of evil intentions. There was also that damn non-discriminating friend who didn't care that Lynn was slightly pudgy; he would nail her anyway. Annica had her share of wingmen make-out sessions from trying to convince me that I was worth more than taking an asshole home. Lynn indulged in her share of non-discriminating friend fucks in the back rocks behind the club. She liked to show me the embedded stones in her knees to prove it. We all got what we wanted, and the guys did too— everyone seemed happy.

Other than the trickery of women versus men and vice versa, it really was up to me to say no; I just didn't. Annica saved me from myself a few times, but I was stubborn and told her to kick rocks too. It was two steps forward and one step back. You can't win them all.

One Sunday after the tears and the smoking session, Annica told me that her friend Steven was coming over. He was the fucker who labeled me gay. She swore up and down that he was cool, and it was a perfect time to meet him because she was sure that we would get along. To my dismay, an hour later he knocked at our door, and after a brief introduction, I excused myself before he had a chance to sit down. I wasn't interested in meeting the likes of him even if Annica approved. I did, however, take note of his thick glasses and very pudgy physique in the brief minute of introductions. This only pissed me off more as I rushed down the hallway to leave because, by all appearances, the guy who judged me was a nerdy fat ass. Those who live in glass houses... well, you know the rest.

After I left, Annica told me that Steven barely waited for the door to shut before he labeled me once again. "Did you see that paperboy hat she was wearing? She is a lesbian with a capital L." But as she explained, he is harmless and invited him to come over again and again. What can I say? She was absolutely right. I did befriend him in the days after our first encounter, and by the weekend I knew he was the queen of denial.

He tried very hard to act straight around me and other soldiers, but the awkwardness behind it actually made it more obvious. I felt he needed to expel this demon so as an obligation to help him come out of the closet I boldly asked his sexual orientation in true Annica fashion. "Steven, you're gay, aren't you?"

"Aren't *you?*" he said as he pulled out my iron from a wall locker and plugged it in.

"I like girls, yes." We set up the board so he could press his uniform in my room and talk.

Steven instantly changed the pitch in his voice and began to swirl in my computer chair as he waited for the iron to heat. Suddenly the letter 'S' became elongated, and a snap of his fingers was added for emphasis to the main point.

"Girl, mossst people can't tell, but I am tired of not being able to be myssself. *snaps* I haven't been able to find anyone like me to chill with. These boys around here are slick. They play games, and I am not down with that hiding bullshit; that's why I am going back to civilian life so I can be myssself. It's hard being me. *snaps*."

It was the beginning of a wonderful friendship. He welcomed my questions about coming out of the closet and going back in it for the military. His mother was very accepting, and he spoke very fondly of her. She was one of those quiet, passive women, sweet as apple pie when I met her. Steven didn't speak to her the same way he began speaking to me though. He cut out the super fag twists and turns as he talked to her. He became a typical adult man speaking to his mother without all the cursing and extensions of the letter s. Every now and then one would slip, but he tried amicably to respect his mother and held back the flaming characteristics I was used to seeing.

Annica already knew of his sexuality but didn't say a word to me. Funny how a chatterbox could hold secrets like that; no wonder they were friends.

When Steven was comfortable enough, he invited Annica and me to jet ski with his red-headed local Provost Marshal boyfriend. The boyfriend was not out and was very pissed off that Steven invited us; however, we went and had a blast. He was pleasant and seemingly had no problem showing affection around Annica and me, but weeks later after much arguing, Steven confessed that it was the day their relationship went downhill.

"He is hiding, girl. I can't be with a man who will make love to me at night and turn around and pretend he doesn't know me in public. He's just a ssscared little bitch is what he is." Then he asked who I was interested in, but I didn't have a name to give him. Relationships with women were not my priority. Lynn knew of my bisexuality and always flirted, but there were too many boys on the weekends. Chasing women didn't cross my mind and besides there wasn't enough time outside of the one night stand drama and screwing no-name privates.

Additionally, I had a steady something going with Franklin. He was my fuck buddy of seven months, and that's literally all we did. He was twenty-five and nearly bald weighing in at 140lbs with three percent body fat. Hardly the guy anyone would suspect me of sleeping with, he was perfect.

We didn't want anyone to know about our little setup, so we asked in code if the other wanted sex and tried to maintain secrecy. I'd walk to his room, where his roommate always answered the door in his tighty-whities.

"Hey is Franklin in? Could you ask him if he wants to play cards please?" I'd peer into the room that they had painted a deep purple to see if he was in fact in. He was a scrawny guy about twenty-five, but he was going bald. I could see his shirtless pink flesh sitting on his bed through the crack of the door in contrast to the purple paint. And that was it, the unbreakable code we made to boldly ask the other for sex— ingenious really. Sometimes we could yell it down the hallway through the loud music, and no one thought anything of it. Franklin didn't even bother to get up from doing whatever he was doing on his bed. He simply instructed his roommate. "Ask her if she wants me to bring my deck!" This was code for "do you have condoms, or should I bring some?" We had it choreographed very well.

"Bring his deck, tell him I'll be in my room and put some god damn pants on." I walked to my room which was several doors down the hall to wait for his knock in less than four minutes.

As soon as the door to my room shut behind him, we attacked each other as if we were lovers in an affair with limited time to share. The tension was high, and no foreplay was needed; just take the clothes off, stick it in and pump, that's the mission. It was always exciting and arousing to have desire like that no matter where it came from and the clothes never seemed to come off fast enough before he entered me. Sometimes he had the condom on already so it would be much less awkward.

He was a small man with a small penis. There is no polite way to put it, but he was my choice for a fuck buddy because a good poke before going to the club usually helped me leave the other boys alone. That's also what it was, a poke. It took longer for us to rip each other's clothes off than it did for him to orgasm. Poor Franklin was a two pump chump; however, ladies and straight gentlemen that's what I liked about him. Our beneficial relationship worked because we gave each other what we needed, no strings attached. Get in, get out, and take the fucking deck with you when you leave.

Around the time of Franklin and his inability to last longer than three minutes, I was still bringing home boys on the weekends and crying about it to Annica. One particular weekend Annica gathered all of our friends up for a big night out figuring the more people to socialize with the less chances of a quick guilty hookup.

Everyone went, and the plan to keep my vagina in my pants worked. Annica still had her infamous wingman make out sessions. Lynn had some new recruit finger her in a dark corner. My neighbor Rick who looked like a living breathing Ken doll hung out with Lynn's friend Melanie at the bar. Steven brought along a straight friend and played pool all night. We danced so long our blisters had blisters. Eventually, the bartender announced it was last call and the final hour was spent trying to convince each person to stay in one spot so we could leave as a group.

Barely sober enough to drive, we piled into my Geo Metro and made the three-block trek back to the barracks. Annica, by surrounding me with buddies, kept me away from the pussy hungry boys. Now it was time to finish up the night with that last beer among friends.

We tried to use our best drunken whispers to talk in the hallways until we all filled into Rick's room where he played Prince CDs and cracked windows for the smoke to filter out. As far as we were all concerned, the after party had begun.

We joked and screamed at the girl getting laid in the other building. She was so loud that we could hear her through our music. This became our new form of entertainment. We all gathered at the windows, squirming for positions to get as many heads out of it as possible and loudly yelled out orgasmic sounds of our own. The chorus of the fake orgy had the barracks guard outside to investigate and pissed him off enough to threaten us with calling our first sergeants. We settled a bit, and it was a bunch of friends partying, very innocently, just soldiers relieving some stress— until somebody started kissing.

One of those god dammed horny soldiers started French kissing the other and eventually taunted me into the slobber frenzy. There was no thinking involved, just a psychedelic dance of mouths where tongues licked other random tongues in a four-way kissing freak show. Annica and the straight friend of Steven's shared that face people get when the joke isn't funny anymore. Lynn stood laughing and mocking Annica's embarrassment. Soon the lighthearted shouts of initial shock turned into *yeah, it's time to leave.*

Then someone said, *No don't leave, join us.* I thought it was Melanie, but it was my voice I heard. Putting her name on it gave me justification to continue even though my actions gave me as much pleasure as an elbow rub. I was going through the drunken motions for absolutely no reason. The agreement to keep my vagina in my pants was in the back pocket of my jeans on the floor in less than two minutes.

During a separate kiss with Steven, I stopped to ask if what we were doing was turning him on. The shared feeling of boring straight sex had us giggling in each other's faces as we pretended to engage in this debauchery. Steven composed himself long enough to explain his desires for Rick as we shielded our whispers from them. But Steven added that he really had to leave because Rick wasn't gay, it wasn't going to happen for him, and he was getting very uncomfortable.

I whispered back, "I'm staying to get to her," and kissed him goodbye. My focus was on Melanie after Steven left. Even during sex with Rick, my intention was always to get back to her. It became my mechanical strategy and, eventually, I pulled

Melanie to the other twin bed across the room so we could be alone.

Why couldn't Rick just watch like a good boy? He obviously wanted Melanie as much as I did because he followed us all over the room. Ultimately the chemistry between them overwhelmed the experience, and I was left out more than not. That was my cue to exit.

I put my shirt over my naked body and peeked out of the open doorway to check the hall. My intention was to hurl myself across the hall, four feet, to my own door and scurry through it to the safety of my bed. To my surprise, Franklin was blocking the doorway, and my head nearly smashed into his huge shining noggin. I jumped and tugged at my t-shirt to cover my naughty bits. He looked down at my hands pulling the bottom of my t-shirt and although I was covered, he knew I was panty-less. "Go put some pants on," he demanded as he looked at me with disgust.

My eyes tried to adjust to the lights from the hall, but they burned from second-hand smoke and smeared makeup. "I'm just having fun. Relax, Frankie. You should join us," I invited and tried to pull him into the room despite his protest.

"You are drunk." He broke free from my grasp and rebalanced himself in the doorway as he crossed his arms.

"I'm not that drunk. I know what I am doing, and I want you, so let's do it." I didn't want him per se, I wanted to feel like someone desired me and he was my only option.

"I'm not going in. You know the door has been open this whole time?" He was right, but Rick had strategically placed his wall lockers just beyond the entrance so he could get some privacy should his roommate need to leave while he was changing. Sure, it was open, but unless you walked in and around the locker, you couldn't see the shenanigans behind it.

In slurred speech, I asked him if he had been watching as I giggled and reiterated how bad I wanted sex.

Truth was I couldn't handle his rejection, so I begged him a bit more before kissing him in the open doorway, caught between the light of the hallway and the darkness of the room. It was familiar and comforting. He pushed away and looked at me intently, even held my head still for a moment as he stared into my glazed eyes, almost romantically. It was the only time he ever looked into me and connected on a level beyond sex. The kiss was amazing too, the passion behind it surprised me, and it allowed me to enjoy, for the first time, his thick, smooth lips.

I wish I knew what he was thinking in the second before he unzipped his pants and fucked me where we stood. Before there was time to be appalled, he finished and tucked himself back into his jeans. He turned and walked straight to his room, never looking back as he yelled, "Go to bed, Janell."

Chapter 5

The Sunday afternoon light beamed through my window just as Annika's lighter flicked, two or three times. She inhaled, exhaled, and looked over to see my discomfort from the interruption of sleep. The sun peeked around my blinds, misting the room with a cheerful afternoon glow yet somehow managed an intensified stream of light over my eye, searing it right through the eyelid. I struggled to shift my head on the pillow to capture an inch of shade. My attempt was unsuccessful.

Annica hummed that infamous three note wordless phrase: tisk-tisk-tisk. Almost everything that needs to be said about disappointment can be grunted or hummed in this way. It means "damn dirty shame," or "no you didn't," without articulation. I looked over to her smoking in her twin bed without glasses which had been slapped to the floor in an effort to find the pack of smokes and lighter on her nightstand.

I grimaced in disgust, moaned, and threw the covers over my head. Annica repeated those little notes accompanied by a synchronized head shake. This was one of the few times where she didn't need to say anything to be loud and clear. She simply inhaled, then exhaled, and tisked me with squinted eyes. I knew what the fuck it meant.

"I know! Shiiit!!" My voice, still scratchy and dry, popped as it tried to kick start itself with the morning. I pulled the covers tighter over my head and faced the wall in shame. Annica laughed and puffed away until she was finished with the cigarette and lit a second one. She enjoyed it slowly as sleep overwhelmed me and carried me off into another dream. The plan for more people to lessen the chances of a guilty hookup was a bullshit strategy that worked about as well as a broken condom. Little attention was given to the rumors of an orgy in the barracks; in fact, I didn't entertain the idea, I dismissed it all together when Steven and I talked of marriage. We just wanted to be ourselves on the most basic level, and we figured the only way to do that was to marry yet lead our own separate gay lives. It made perfect sense to us.

The agreement was to marry sometime in December if I didn't find anyone else more convincing as a straight man. We would be two gay roommates essentially, and no one would be the wiser. The money would be better and the freedom, priceless. We hung out more and took lots of photos to portray a budding relationship. I listened to details of his life and noted the little things he did to deceive the masses. However, there were things he just couldn't hide, like the curved shape his fingers made when he pressed on the volume button to listen to Erasure. Of course, my version of our story replaced the artist and omitted his squeals of excitement over the lyric "In the fields where poppies grow." That was the plan. It was the summer of '97, the supposed beginning of my hidden lesbian life.

Melanie held my affections after the sex fest in the barracks. I gave her attention, helped her pick out weekend outfits, bought her simple gifts, listened to her talk about Rick, and asked, with genuine concern, how her new diet was going even though she was perfect. She always thanked me with a wink and a smile when I complimented her.

Unashamed

During this infatuation for Melanie I remember my mother calling me and how, for the second time, I tried to come out of the closet. A bulky cordless phone allowed me to walk and talk to the day room, which is a common entertainment area for soldiers to use. In it was a television, couch, pool table, chairs, a card table, and general items to keep soldiers entertained. I passed Melanie's room on my way there and noticed her door was ajar. And by that, I truly mean wide open. So, of course, I slowed my pace and looked in. She was inside laughing and joking with a friend on her twin bed. When she saw me pass by, she made her way to the door, curious as to where I was going. She watched me walk all the way down the hall with the phone to my ear. Just before I turned into the dayroom, I stopped and twisted around to look back. We stared at each other at opposite ends of the hallway and smiled as hard as we both could smile. I'm sure I was blushing as my heart swelled. Her friend came to the doorway, curious to see what distracted Melanie. Both of them smiled at me. My mother was talking to me, but I heard Melanie's friend ask *is that her* before they giggled. Then she waved at me to come over, but I gestured to her that I was on the phone. As I looked at her and she looked at me beyond her friend's head, I just said it without thought.

"Mom, I think I am gay. I like girls." There were no feelings of nervousness or worry about how Mom would accept it. It fell out of my mouth regardless of her potential reaction. Can you imagine my poor mother talking about making potato soup from scratch when I hit her with *hey I'm a homosexual?* She wasn't ready. She wasn't ready.

I twinkled my fingers to Melanie, and she returned the gesture. It made her smile harder, and she nervously crossed her arms to giggle again. Her friend hit her shoulder and dragged her back into the room. They laughed loudly before the door slammed shut.

Mom sighed like she was giving me tax advice. "Stop it. Geez, lots of women experiment, that doesn't mean you are gay."

"Well, I must be bisexual then because I like girls a lot. I mean, really like girls, Mom," I said still smiling. I was not paying attention to the words that slipped from my mouth into my mother's ears. It all just flowed so easily. "What if I *am* gay?" I asked as I turned from the hallway to enter the dimly lit dayroom. There was no need for lights as I plopped myself on the couch.

"Stop saying that," she demanded. "Yer not gay. You are having fun experimenting, but you better knock it off because it's a lustful thing. Don't worry about it. It's just something yer going' through," she added.

I laughed at her and rolled my eyes like most defiant children do. "Mom, it's not a phase I keep telling you that. It hasn't gone away since eighth grade!" I shrieked like I did after hearing a good dirty joke. "But okay, Mom…" I rolled my eyes again.

After my laughing subdued, she didn't know what to say so for a moment she gave pause then started to hit me with some hard-hitting gospel. "You better start reading your Bible."

This additional last-ditch effort to terminate the conversation and move on only made me throw my head back against the couch in minor frustration. "I know, Sodom and Gomorrah, I know."

Her reaction to my reference was to educate me on the biblical truth. "*Yes!* God banished the homosexuals into two cities of sinners. One for the men and one for the women—"

I didn't let her finish; I simply cut her off. "Oh my God, Mom, I *know!*" Then we both fell quiet because we were finished talking about this unholy subject. Mom ended the conversation with the childhood nickname mothers make up out of love; the name that doesn't make any sense and makes their kid's skin crawl when spoken. Only mine wasn't made from love it was made from some kind of inside joke that I will never be privy to. "Well Fungus I love you, but I'm going to go."

"I love you too Mom but stop calling me Fungus." And we pleasantly hung up the phone as if a typical conversation had just taken place. I walked back to my room and mumbled to myself *Fungus... What the fuck does that mean anyway?*

Days later when I felt the time was right, I talked to Melanie about dating me. I assured her no one would know. This was a bold move, yet I was comfortable asking face to face. I don't know why really. In 1997 it certainly wasn't acceptable nor was it approved of in the military under the Don't Ask, Don't Tell policy. This policy was put in place prior to my entry into the Army to allow people, regardless of their sexual preferences, to serve in the military. Half of the rule was that others couldn't ask a person about their sexuality; the other was that you didn't talk about it. If you did, it was grounds for reprimand and potentially getting kicked out of the service just by asking or telling. So, there was that. But I wasn't thinking about policies. I asked her out face to face because I just liked a girl and I hoped that she liked me too.

She actually surprised me in saying that she liked both me and Rick but felt something serious was developing between the two of them. She apologized while touching my hair and told me how pretty I was at the same time.

For some reason, I didn't take this as rejection. I was sincerely not wanted as much as someone else, and it was okay with me. Internally, I knew that I couldn't win them all and really, the act of asking a girl to date me was accomplishing something far more than getting the wanted answer. It did, however, take a while for me to stop thinking she would change her mind. It hurts when you are not the chosen one.

The first girl to express anger from *my* rejection came from my straight man-loving friend Lynn. I had no clue she was even interested in me until the night she had a little too much to drink and asked me to talk to her in the bathroom. She was upset because she had been trying to show interest in me and just wanted to know if I found her attractive. When I gently explained that I only saw her as my friend she became wild with anger. After calming her down, she suddenly grabbed my head and pressed her face to mine as I tried to pull away. I tightened my lips, squeezed my eyes, and attempted to take a step back which sent me flying into the wall behind the bathroom door. She called me a bitch and continued screaming obscenities at me as she jerked open the door to leave. As if the door nearly hitting my face wasn't enough, her final dig was calling me a fucking dyke as she took off her shoes and threw them down the hall toward her room. Her feet slowly slapped the tiles as she stumbled and sobbed. It hurt her not to be the chosen one.

I ran back to tell Annica about rejecting Lynn and in true Annie style, she tisked me while she smoked her cigarette.

Rejection from the same sex wasn't the only kind I experienced in the early days of sexual discovery. It was apparent that Franklin and I didn't really like each other outside of our little pokey poke sessions. Matter of fact, he explicitly told me once that he was with me because he was waiting on 'the one' and once she came along, I was going to be tossed aside like an old hat. Tired of being his cum rag, I made it seem like a tragic love tale as I told him to go fuck himself with pleasant, lovely words of course. No more playing cards with Franklin's small deck. Realistically we didn't respect each other enough to watch a movie in the day room let alone share quality time on a date, so I lost no sleep over that rejection. In fact, I slept very well that night and even took a nap the next afternoon. I don't know how long I was out before the phone rang and shot me out of bed so fast, I became dizzy. I answered hello in that deep-just-woke-up-clearing-your-vocal-cords kind of way. The man on the other end said my name with question.

My head cocked to the side inquisitively as I rubbed the corner of my eye with my finger. It sounded so familiar, yet I wasn't fully awake, so nothing triggered the identity of the man on the other end. For a split second, I thought I knew who it was, but it couldn't be.

"This is Robert," As soon as he said it the internal voice in my head screamed *holy fuck you were right*. Robert waited to speak again because he certainly knew his call would turn my life upside down. To this day there is just no other way to explain how I nearly shit a brick. Like physically managed to formulate a hard, heavy square concrete object in my colon and let it rip through my asshole before it dropped to the ground with a thud. Luckily my butt hole puckered, and I can only say I nearly shit a brick when my first love called me.

He finally broke the silence but spoke without proper sentence breaks to prevent me from interjecting. "I'm not with my daughter's mother anymore, and I know this is totally out of the blue. Um, your mom gave me your number, I hope its ok.

Anyway, I never stopped loving you. I still love you, and I just thought we could talk."

I'll admit, I was very glad he called despite everything. We caught up on the past two years and ended the call on a positive note. I actually had plans to return to my hometown for a wedding. "Do you remember Sunny from junior high? She's getting married, and I already bought the tickets so I could attend her wedding. If you want Robert, I would like to see you," I said

He answered back, "I'd like that."

After my arrival in Ohio in the summer of 1997, I became swept up in the circle of innocence surrounding my first love all over again. All the things I loved about him as a teenager were still the same with additional maturity and the drive to be a better man. He was working insane hours, taking care of his daughter during his visitation and building a house on his own time. Yet he managed to squeeze me into his busy schedule and attend the wedding with me. I was convinced he was the man I could spend the rest of my life with and was willing to take on the role as a loving step-mother to his child.

I didn't worry about Steven or our plans to be married so we could protect our lives as gay soldiers. I was in love with my high school sweetheart. I felt like the feeling had never left me and never would. Therefore, it was only right to begin our engagement on the week I was home. The plan was for him to move to Arizona with me and be married in December. Our only major concern was the decision he had to make about gaining full-time custody of his daughter or to give it up for our new life together.

Lovestruck choices led him to give me an engagement chain he had worn since junior high. We figured the rings would come soon enough. He claimed he never took it off, not even to shower and that it was now mine to symbolize our newly established status as a couple. I cried as he gently placed it around my neck before we made love for the first time. He was the missing piece in my heart. He was a worker, a protector, a best friend, and a wonderful father.

Robert accepted my underlying bisexuality, but we never talked about it in depth. The only time it was mentioned was when we dropped off his daughter at her mother's apartment. I was overwhelmed with the way it had all worked out between Robert, his ex, and me. She got what she gave in full circle, and I was secretly gloating over how ironic a turn the love triangle had taken.

I wanted her to see me sitting next to her daughter in the truck with Robert by my side. She caused me so much anguish on my living room floor that it wasn't necessary to say a word to her. I remained speechless as we drove into the complex to meet her outside.

She was initially shocked to see me. It hurt her in a way that only the situation could provide. To me, it was worth every second to let her sort out her anger and disgust right in front of my smiling face. I sat quietly as they talked through the window about times for the next visit and argued about losing pacifiers.

When a friend of hers began to approach the car, I shifted uneasily in my seat thinking, surely, they would respect a child's presence and avoid physical violence. But this was white trash I was dealing with. Who knew if this girl had pre-made a shank in her hand with my name on it?

I never caught the girl's name, but I remember her stares and accusations vividly. Without hesitation, she walked over to my window, glared at me very mechanically and without emotion. She lingered in the moment, making it more uncomfortable than if she would have just punched me in the tit, causing me to gasp for air and ensuring a future fifteen minutes of fame on Jerry Springer.

She looked to Roberts' baby momma through the open windows in the vehicle. "Is this the bitch you talked to on the phone?" She asked, referring to a quick conversation gone wrong the day before.

"That's fucking her." the ex said as she stood at the driver's side window.

"She's not even cute." Her face turned quizzical as she spoke to the ex on the other side like my presence was nonexistent. "Are you a dyke? I heard you were a dyke." She finally directed her comment right at me.

All attention was diverted to my response. The ex stopped to listen. Robert looked over to me while the baby sucked on her sippy-cup. The friend crossed her arms as I said *no* partially smiling in embarrassment, shock, and amazement at anyone knowing anything about my life in Arizona or Angel. The look on my face, I'm sure, was priceless. The rest of the shitty time spent in judgmental hillbilly hell was just as unpleasant. When we finally left, there wasn't much to say to each other.

The ex must have relished in the moment as her friend waved to us on our way out, "See you later, ya fuckin' dyke!"

When we didn't see them in the side mirrors anymore, I nervously said, "What was that all about? God. Did you say anything to her about me?"

"I was with her a long time. I told her things." He wasn't exactly sorry, but he felt bad for it coming up when it was never meant to go beyond the ex's ears.

"Jesus Robert, that's my business!" I said with a passive, hurt, betrayed exclamation point at the end of the sentence.

"Don't worry about it. She knows about my experiments with that guy from work and tells everyone I am a fag. Everyone experiments. I'm not gay. No one believes anything she says anyway," he assured me as he looked to me with his brilliant blue eyes then back to the road.

I began talking to him and to myself as we passed corn fields that created a distinct yet indefinable smell. I didn't look at him; rather I mesmerized myself with the rows and rows of corn that was still too young to be harvested. "I can't believe it. Did you hear that? How she just said it? A dyke." I contemplated that thought and that word as it replayed in my head. Seems I'd been called that a lot lately; am I?

I let the neatly lined rows of corn pass before my eyes as I visually blended it all together making a green haze. I sat there swirling it all in my mind, and for a second, I thought: I don't want to marry him, I'm gay.

Within the first week of my return to Arizona military life, I talked to Robert about the people we were seeing before our decision to be married. We agreed that in the months before our anticipated wedding we would be free to have sexual relationships with others to get it out of our systems. We understood our young bodies couldn't place sex on hold. States divided us physically but never our love. My heart knew where it belonged and where it had been since the day of his earth-shattering lie in my living room. I was ready to commit myself to him for the rest of my life, and together we joked about our last few months of getting it on with those who would never know the depth of our devotion.

I was boastful of my renewed love for Robert and showed anyone who would take interest my engagement chain. Steven accepted his future bride to be was just another bisexual girl returning to the security of a normal heterosexual world. He was happy for me, but I noticed we did not hang out like we used to after my announcement. I pushed everyone out who didn't understand my decision.

Steven faded from my life, but I barely noticed.

Chapter 6

My new roommate, a Jamaican girl, born in California, insisted on telling me how nuts I was about the whole thing. She didn't know my sexuality like Annica did. In her mind, the barracks hoe was suddenly getting married but still sleeping around. No wonder Tenesa kept her distance.

She didn't say anything when I brought home this quiet virgin boy and two nights later slept with his squad leader, who'd I known from basic training. She never asked me about the tall, dark, handsome guy from the chow hall or the French, Tori Amos fan. She let my business be my business and never intervened until the evergreen incident when the drunken French guy came into our room while she was sleeping. He shook her awake to ask if he could sleep in my bed. She knew I was down the hall with the freckle-faced boy and his amazing red hair.

Tenesa asked me never to put her in that situation again as she explained how Frenchie begged her in the dark to stay. He apparently showed her the scratches and green skid marks on his body from earlier in the night when he tried to climb an evergreen tree outside of my window to reach me and fell to the rocks.

Tenesa, in a California version of her Jamaican accent, reported, "Dis boy was cryin' so hard. He totally smelled like beer and eva-green fuckin' bush or some shit, girl." We laughed at the stupidity of the story as we got ready to go clubbing and listened to the messages he left on my machine. Sober at first, just saying hello then progressing through his drunkenness into anger and tears. It was sadly hysterical, this poor guy was lovestruck over me, and I had plans to marry.

Tenesa kept her judgments to herself and never made any mention of how I was living my life. But it's always the quiet ones who have the most to say. She would have given me an earful if she was sure I would listen but to her, but I was a lost cause, and she was focused on her night classes at the local college. The last thing on her mind was trying to save me from myself.

The second time she brought up my promiscuity was when she had plans to drive with this boy from her class to California in search of a new car. It certainly wasn't out of concern with my behavior; it was more for her sanity and safety when she returned. Another Frenchie, midnight wakeup call was not going to be tolerated again. As she neatly packed a bag on the opposite side of the barracks room, she casually asked and told me at the same time, to give it a rest. "Listen, girl; I'm driving with dis white boy to California and bringing back a car. So, I'll be on leave for two weeks. Could you get out all ya fuckin' before I get back?"

I dismissed the idea with a wave of my hand and told her I was done sleeping around because I was getting married. As if it was actually that simple. She didn't believe a fucking word I said.

While she was gone, I put my hands up in the air and backed away from my struggles with sexual orientation so I could focus on my upcoming unity with Robert. We talked every day on the phone about our future and how exciting it was to rekindle our childhood romance. We discussed his daughter and finances and practical things that go along with moving and procedures for getting married. I felt our love was so transcendent that I sat through a painful session in a local tattoo parlor to get his initials permanently etched into my skin.

And then, the next morning while happily checking and washing my new ink, I was hit with the reality of bumps on my genitals. Sexual flamboyancy is a time bomb ticking away and one day, boom; you explode with a disease. All you can do is hope and pray that it's not something that lasts a lifetime or worse. If anything kicks a person in the teeth to the realities of promiscuity, it's a venereal disease. Additionally, mine appeared right after the decision was made to stop my shenanigans. I almost made it without getting burned. The following morning the doctor immediately diagnosed me with genital warts. The first few days I was disgusted with myself, but I knocked on Josh's door, telling him to come to my room as soon as possible. He had to be told.

He came in; I shut the door and didn't hesitate springing the news for fear that I would lose my nerve. We were alone but the subject matter was so serious that I spoke at the lowest volume possible, yet I was very matter of fact. "Look, I went to the doctor, and the last person I was with was you so I think you should get checked out because I have genital warts. I wanted to tell you because I think you gave them to me."

There we stood in the middle of my room staring at each other, blinking, not knowing what to do or say. I hadn't realized how unattractive he truly was until that moment. Freckles, which were cute in the beginning, covered his entire body but under the circumstances they just made his skin look dirty. His teeth were yellow and coated in what appeared to be a thick layer of plaque. The t-shirt he wore was stretched out and slightly grey. I'm not sure if he showered regularly, but he sprayed enough cologne on to choke a horse. I wondered how I could overlook those things and engage in sex with this animal. This was definitely an eye-opener to the standards I had been setting for myself.

After he stared at me with deer in the headlight glare, he shook his freckled face in disbelief then squinted as if to shoot daggers at me with those green beady eyes. "You didn't get them from me," he said bluntly. "I know you sleep around."

Let me tell you how wonderful it feels to have a freckle-faced, bumpy dick mother fucker, tell you that *you* are the virus carrying slut. Not so much. Yet, I was trying to be the bigger person so I remained calm and explained the situation before I could panic and slap the red out of his hair. "The last guy I was with was a week before you, and the doctor says it takes three days for it to appear which means it's *you* because *you* were the last one that I was with three days ago. And really that's not the fucking point. Just go get checked out before you spread it around. I'm trying to set aside my embarrassment by telling you and doing you a favor, ok." By the end, my anger had escalated, but my restraint was impeccable.

When he left, I felt relieved that I'd done my good deed for the week, even if it meant undue shame. And so began my pills and weekly visits to a military doctor for topical treatments; to say the least, it definitely aided in my transition to becoming a little less sexual.

When Tenesa came back, she was sporting super tight braids and a renewed Jamaican accent that was heavier than when she left. After unpacking, Tenesa cried in pain as she tried to lay her head on her pillow and was unable to do so. Her hair was so tight she had to sit against the wall to finish her story about the white boy who accompanied her and how funny he was the whole trip.

Tenesa spoke of his glasses and how nerdy he was as she prepared to sleep seated in that position. The funny part was Tenesa said she had to sleep like that before due to some "tight Jamaican bray-den." She assured me she would be able to sleep normally in a few days.

Every comment of hers was a shot of happy energy to my sad soul. I wanted to listen to everything that happened on her trip even though we had never really had much of a conversation before. I could tell that my enthusiastic demeanor over her stories served as intangible shots of happy energy for her too.

Between laughing at her tales of woe and the agony of her "Jamaican bray-den," I teased that she must really like this guy because she couldn't stop talking about him. Tenesa insisted that she was not into white boys, but if she was, this kid would interest her. We cracked jokes about black and white love, making references to all possible clichés. For once, the weird hostility between us relaxed. It could have been the pain that subdued her, but it was nice to chat and make her laugh even if it snapped her head back to the only comfortable position she could find. Her misery as she gently placed her hand on her braids was amusing to me because she winced every time, yet she kept doing it. After a while, it wasn't funny anymore because as she pointed out, it was so tight that each hair on her head was about to pop out of the embedded root of her scalp. She was very serious as she sat upright and still on her mattress to catch a fleeting pain-free moment. Very slowly she articulated, "The only other time... my head felt dis way was... when... some nigglett ripped out a braid... he left a bald throbbin' empty square patch."

With my hand over my mouth, I tried not to laugh, but I exploded and cackled so loud and hard that I sprayed the inside of my hand with spit before my face turned three shades of purple. Thank god she laughed too, well she tried not to. I believe this was the first time Tenesa and I had a good conversation; it was therapeutic really. We talked for quite some time about the white boy, her family, my tattoo, and how her boyfriend got mad when she broke things off with him for some guy she met in the Army. The boyfriend's quote was, *Who this nigga Nees-a? I'll knock his blackness back to Aff-ree-ka.* This last comment and delivery of it threw us into hysterics before I tuckered out and fell to sleep.

The shame that accompanied pills and weekly visits to the doctor became a burden I couldn't bear. I had four bumps that refused to go away. It was enough to drive me to into a self-loathing cleaning frenzy; one shower after physical training, one at lunch, another after work, and my last one just before bed. All were attempts to decontaminate my skin and rid my mind of the terrible infliction. I was trapped within my revolting body.

So, on my last visit to the doctor, I begged the attendant to give me the damn chemical, so I could burn the fucking things off myself. That is how I asked for it too.

I explained my excessive cleaning routine and how it was becoming painful (not to mention the most horrible experience) to see a new person every clinical visit. The soldier, who must have been my age, left the room and came back minutes later with a new bottle. It was tucked into his sleeve like we were doing a drug deal, trying not to get busted by the pigs. He told me to use it once every other day to speed up the process of removal.

When I left the clinic, I was practically skipping with joy. That little vial in the bottom of the brown paper bag was my new savior. I ran down the hall to take a shower and put the chemical on myself in the toilet stall when I was sure no one was around.

Nothing could have made me happier than the wart remover in my possession.

I decided that the pain was worth getting me back to normal again, so I exceeded the attendant's advice and used the chemical three times a day, holding my fists against the stall walls to cope with the burning, not making a sound. With each application, I broke a sweat when the chemical absorbed into delicate skin unaffected by any disease. I would come out of the stall in pain, in tears, and drained from enduring what I was doing to rid my body of this problem.

Sex was a distant disgusting memory with either gender. I didn't go anywhere or see anybody or make phone calls to Robert. No one knew what I was going through physically and surely no one, but another person who has been through a venereal disease, can understand what it does mentally. All day, every day, I was tortured by how disgusted I was with myself or how embarrassing it was being stuck in my afflicted body.

Every shower or bathroom visit became my own purgatory. I was reminded visually and tactically that the bumps were still there. It was all I could think about for over a month each time I shifted in my chair at work. It became my small insanity and, eventually, I couldn't handle them being there anymore.

So, I pulled and cut off two remaining warts with fingernail clippers.

I had prepared the clippers with rubbing alcohol and burned the clipping edge with my lighter for more sterility, hoping it would make a cleaner cut. My nerves had me shaking uncontrollably, but I managed to hold in a scream that would have shattered the mirrors above the sinks. My fists pressed so hard against the stall partitions my knuckles drained white. When I couldn't hover over the toilet anymore, I leaned forward holding my weight with my head against the door and let loose with my emotions and cried so hard I could barely breathe. Still, I remained quiet, and when I somewhat composed myself, I walked with numbed agony to my room and went to bed.

This was truly punishment for my behavior, and that I should thank God for the simple discomfort I felt rather than a devastating disease I could have earned. After cutting myself off (no pun intended) from men, I focused on healing.

I rested even when Lynn and Annica were knocking on my door asking me to go dancing at the Ozone. I became a hermit of sorts; watching Tenesa fix her braids in preparation for a night at the club while I made up some lie to keep me inside. Everyone noticed the change in me, but nobody pried.

It was during one of these party weekends when I finally met the white boy. While everyone went out, Tenesa opted to stay in so she could prepare for an exam. I was already tucked into my bed, enjoying a smoke and reading a magazine when at the last minute Tenesa announced that the white boy was coming over to help her study for psychology. However, I didn't even have time to put a bra on before his knock rapped at our door. We both shouted in unison that it was ok to enter. The door partially opened and a guy poked his head in. From the angle of my bed to the door I saw thick dark hair and big chocolate brown eyes. I immediately pulled the covers up a little to cover my nipples which anyone could see through the nightshirt. When the guy walked in his six foot two stature surprised me as well as his thick and wavy Spanish hair that was kept short and his Greek god smile. My first thought was *holy fuck he is hot* which immediately preceded *he is not fucking white*.

While I was embarrassed by my sheep print pajamas, he could have cared less. His concern was his immediate reaction to the smoke in the room and how it was burning his eyes. His arms flailed in front of his face to fan it, but it caught him off guard, and he coughed anyway. Then he forced a few more coughs for dramatic effect. I made some stupid nervous comment about our infamous purple haze room before I opened the window behind my bed for his comfort. As he sat in a chair in the middle of the room unpacking his books, I stared like how a baby stares when they see something sparkling.

He was sexy, and it blew my mind as to the reasons Tenesa referred to him as white. Sure, his skin was white, but he was exotic looking with thick lips, unlike any typical American Ken doll replica I had ever seen.

Observing his hair, eyes, and widened nose, I asked, "What's your background? Because this skank has been calling you a white boy for weeks."

His frank reply was, "I'm Mediterranean." Then he laughed as he pushed his glasses up onto the bridge of his nose and pulled a notebook and pen from his bag. He balanced the notebook on the arm of the chair and clipped the pen neatly within the coiled binding. He covered his mouth and respectfully excused himself after another cough then he proceeded to remove the glasses from his face to clean each lens with the bottom of his shirt. The way he reset them on his face for a second time and pushed them perfectly to the bridge of his nose was slightly pompous.

My mouth was open in disbelief the whole time. "Oh my God, who says that? Are you kidding... Mediterranean?" I looked to Tenesa for confirmation that I wasn't the only one who thought that it was odd. We both rolled our eyes at each other.

He snickered like this wasn't the first time he had been berated with questions about his ethnicity. He shot us both a crooked nervous smile before patiently explaining that his mother was Spanish and Italian, and his father was Spanish and German but that it was far easier to say Mediterranean than to explain all that every time someone asked about his heritage.

I placed my pillow against the ledge of the window so I could sit against it. He was interesting enough to want to hear more and hot enough to want more in general. "Can't you just pick two of them like a normal person would?" I mocked with flirtatious undertones.

Tenesa laughed and lifted one of her braids but forgot it was still tight; she sucked in air through her teeth in pain. "Jamaican American, that's my two."

I pressed my index finger to my collar bone. "German American."

He pointed his index finger to his right eye, just above the rim of his glasses. His eyes grew wide, and his smile began to take over the bottom half of his face. "Well, I am Medi-fucking-terranean." He said as he tilted his head in the opposite direction with every syllable.

Three of us laughed, but he laughed so hard he coughed again. When everything calmed down, he finally officially introduced himself with a proper handshake, eye contact, and articulation. I remained in my bed with the covers discretely covering the see-through sheep as I shook his hand. "I'm Douglas, nice to meet you. Since *some*body isn't a very gracious host." He shot a glare at Tenesa who was smiling and shrugging her shoulders. I held his hand longer than what was required. I deduced that his job definitely did not require serious manual labor.

He returned to the seat in the middle of the room with my twin to his left and Tenesa's bed on his right. They studied for their exam between storytelling and thunderous bursts of laughter. Eventually, it was nearing an uncomfortably late hour and time for him to leave.

I waited until I couldn't hear his footsteps anymore before I shrieked, "Tenesa, he's not white, you asshole! Oh my God, he is so fucking hot! Here I have been thinking this guy is a dork with glasses and pimples all over his face. Jesus!" I lit a cigarette as I remained in my seated position against the window.

She carefully set her books into her bag, awkwardly pushing them to the bottom without moving her head too much. "He's a white boy to me." She zipped up the bag and pushed it off of the bed, so she didn't have to bend down.

"And you are not interested in him?" I asked in disbelief as I struggled to crack the window with my free hand.

She grabbed a small bottle of something from her nightstand and squeezed a glob of it into the center of her hand. "I told you I don't like white boys." With her other hand, she dipped two fingers in the glob then smeared it on her scalp between each braid. Her body relaxed as she closed her eyes and rubbed the thick liquid in.

I flicked the ashes into an ashtray on my nightstand. "Well shit if you don't want him, I'll take him. He is totally sexy," I rambled on about Douglas for another twenty minutes and two cigarettes later before she finally told me to shut the hell up so she could sleep.

Well, so she could rest her head against the wall and at least try it.

In the weeks following this initial meeting with the "white boy," I maintained contact with my fiancé back in Ohio. We continued to talk about things in a practical sense while Tenesa's braids loosened enough to let her sleep on an actual pillow.

One night Tenesa told me that she wanted to have her new boyfriend spend the night and pressured me to disappear. A favor she said for putting up with the creeps that kept coming around.

"Where am I supposed to go?" I asked, feeling obligated to kick rocks and sleep somewhere else for the night.

Miraculously her phone rang as if God himself heard me. It was Douglas, the Mediterranean, calling to see what she was doing. She boldly asked him without hesitation if I could stay at his place just for the night as a favor. He said yes and was on his way to pick me up in fifteen minutes. I ran straight to the showers to shave my legs, just in case.

Douglas' room was physically cold but warm in the way he decorated it as if he was in some fancy Italian hotel room. I was shocked at the luxurious comforter neatly made up on his bed and lavish looking tapestries were hanging on the shabby barracks walls. This "white boy" had style. Displayed proudly on the desk was a photo of his family at a wedding which reminded me of aristocratic portrait taken in Spain soon after the invention of the camera when only the wealthy could afford such things.

My family photos consisted of my dad, mom, sister and me at JC Penny's where, at five, I was smiling like Mickey Mouse with noticeable dirt behind my ear. My red-headed sister hadn't gone through major eye surgery yet, so she was unaware of her severe crossed eyes behind Coke bottle glasses but smiled despite that and her overcrowded teeth. My family, on both sides, had photos like this. They were typical for the decade, quantity versus quality. Grandparents on both sides received huge 8 x 10's and wallet sized pictures. Aunts and uncles had to buy 5 x 7 frames and crop the 2 x 4's to fit into their purses. Friends were given the credit card photos to pushpin to their bulletin boards at work.

Everyone else had to squint to see the dirt behind my ear in the photos glued into cheap quarter size pendants.

Douglas' family photos were beyond JC Penny pendants. His were printed on very expensive ribbed canvas and framed in a cherry wood embossed design. I was so impressed I never had time to take in the leather couch he had placed strategically to create space for a living room. The focal point was a large entertainment center holding all the electronics necessary to boom Tori Amos into the room.

He played a techno rendition of a familiar song on repeat just because I mentioned I was a fan of her music. He was a classy guy all right, but I know he was being a smooth operator and really just wanted to taste my rainbow.

He tried to be slick by letting me know that if I were to get too cold on the couch, I was more than welcome to sleep with him on his very small twin bed. I smirked through the dark where I lay on the couch with one foot hanging over the edge.

I almost took him up on the offer. I felt that surge of energy needed to push oneself up from the cold leather but remained still, content that I was finally sticking to my proclamation. We didn't say anything else as we fell to sleep in our own comfortable spaces.

The next morning, when I returned early to my barracks room Tenesa's new boyfriend had gone, but his smell remained, and I don't mean his cologne. She was lying on her bed flipping through a magazine when I walked in. She turned her head when I opened the door, but she never looked over with her eyes. "Didja git lucky?" She said and licked her finger before turning another page.

As I tossed my keys onto my mattress and kicked my shoes off, I said, "I did. I slept on the couch." The smirk on my face was that of achievement.

Every time I saw Douglas in the week following our sleepover it was at the chow hall; he made military food taste good to me. I was excited to get up in the morning and be alive another day just to see him.

We sat together in our own booth. My group of guy friends looked on and nudged each other, thinking that this kid was just another conquest. In our gang of eight, I was the only female, so the boys felt like it was their duty to look after me no matter what kind of wild child I had become. In the months of sitting at our regular table three times a day we all became very close so with one space empty, we'd know someone was spitting game to get laid. Well, with the exception of one guy. He was getting married and had to undergo taunts and jokes with the occasional punches in the arm all in the name of brotherly love. The nudges the boys gave each other as we sat sometimes accompanied a thumbs-up hand gesture or the motion of sucking dick with hysterical laughter.

Just because I was the only girl didn't mean leniency from teasing. I would scrunch my lips with the wide-eyed stare that moms give to their kids at the mall when they are misbehaving. You know, the look that will stop a kid cold through a crowd and somehow by forces unknown draw him back to the mother with a sulking head. This is when she would proceed to escort him to the door by the neck and beat his ass at the car. As soon as I knew Douglas was looking at me again, I would smile and seem glorious much like the mother's expression would be after returning to the mall to finish her Christmas shopping.

Each time I sat with Douglas and left an empty chair at my usual table, the boys would shrug and point to my seat as if to say, *What the fuck? Are you ever coming back or what? We miss you.* Eventually, they didn't bother us in our little booth, off in our own little world. Maybe I just didn't notice. I was in la-la land with him, totally smitten yet reserved because I did not think he would ever give me the time of day. I felt like he was someone who would never date me simply because he was just too good looking and far too intelligent to be interested in the barracks hoe.

But then one day, before I turned the corner to leave the lunchroom, he shouted from his booth. "Hey, do you want to go to this club with me and some friends this weekend?"

I turned in shock, my head cocked to the side, and I paused for a moment a complete skeptic. From across the noisy chow hall, I stood in the exit with my jaw to the floor. Even as we smiled at each other, I thought he was joking. I blinked a lot before shouting back, "Sure."

When I entered the chow hall, I was on foot, but when I left, I was floating on a cloud.

Impressed with him in every way I was further awestruck by his car. How cliché right? It wasn't some fancy speed racer that caught my eye. It was that he had a top of the line *new* car that still smelled and looked like it had just rolled off of the sales lot. The interior and trunk weren't just clean; they were immaculate.

Intimidated by this I wondered how I would fit into his expensive world. But I felt stately as I got in and smiled while introducing myself to the couple seated in the back. Terrance shook my hand first as he said, "Yeah I know you. What's up, girl?" Then he squeezed my shoulder in friendly recognition.

"Oh my god T, you know Douglas?" My eyes shifted from Terrance's smile in the back to Doug adjusting the rearview mirror in the driver's seat. Admittedly, I was confused as to how they might know each other because they were so different. Terrance was a hardcore party animal who frequented raves. Not that Douglas couldn't party, but he just seemed to be in control of things and very responsible. Club kids and studious college students don't usually hang in the same crowds.

"Yeah girl, this here is my boy! The pimp!" He said as he shook the headrest on Douglas's seat then scuffed the top of his head. Douglas immediately began to fix his hair in the mirror, but he didn't seem pissed; he was smiling.

I knew Terrance from the club where we were friendly dance partners a few times. The weekend prior I had given him a lift when he was too drunk to shake his lanky ass anymore. He squeezed his 6' 3" frame into my Geo Metro the best he could without throwing up, and I dropped him off at his barracks. "So, what happened after I dropped you off from the bar?" I shifted in my seat to see him more clearly.

Terrance pushed back into his seat and began to buckle his seat belt. "I went to bed and knocked the fuck out. Didn't get up 'till about fo thirty the next day." He clicked it tight and put his arm around the girl sitting next to him.

Doug interjected to ask me. "You know this fool?"

"Yeah, he got ripped at the bar, so I took him to his barracks last week. He was dancing like he was having seizures."

I laughed as Terrance used his free hand to nervously exaggerate his embarrassment. "Please don't tell these things." He removed his arm from behind the girls' neck and folded them over his crotch. Not only was he a tall, skinny black man but this was the first time I took notice of how fidgety he was. "I'm losing all my cool points and shit. It wasn't even like that man; it's all lies!" Terrance nervously giggled then leaned forward between the seats to change the CD. "Let's go already. I'm gettin' a fucking cramp in my black ass back here."

We let Terrance dominate the first 15 minutes of travel conversation. He provided the ice breaking we all needed so by the time we arrived in Tucson we were behaving like best friends.

I'd been surprised that Douglas, with all his portrayals of sophistication, would be buddies with a down to earth, slightly ghetto kid like Terrance. It definitely helped sooth my comfort level and showed me another side of Douglas the great Italiano magnifico— I mean "Medi-fucking-terranean."

After having a few drinks at the hotel room, the four of us walked to the club. After having a few drinks at the club Douglas and I walked back to the hotel.

I figured it would be better to have sex in private than to have his hands in my pants on the dance floor, although no one was actually looking. I was wet, and this was rare in itself, so I whispered in his ear, *"Let's go back to the room."*

Without hesitation, we left our drinks behind right along with Terrance and the girl he came with. On the short walk back, he held my hand smiling. It was a genuinely happy smile, unlike the greedy, lustful faces I was accustomed to seeing. I thought he was absolutely the sexiest man I'd ever met without a shadow of a doubt. I wanted to sleep with him and so it happened.

I cannot tell you how long it actually lasted or how wonderful it was because my first time with Douglas wasn't about the sex. I actually can't remember that part. It was all of the things before the encounter and all of the things after it that made me fall in love with him.

Afterward, I rested in his arms for hours as if we had been together for years. We talked and joked and laughed the entire time before deciding to really make an effort to fall asleep. In the morning we were the happiest couple. We dove into conversation as soon as we realized the other was awake. When an hour passed Douglas got up to pee as I brushed my teeth at the sink, then he stepped into the shower as I took my turn on the toilet, quite naturally choreographed.

I pointed out a fact as I wiped the urine off of my body and flushed. "Jesus, look at us, we have not stopped talking. You would think we were married! I'm peeing in front of you for God's sake. I never do that!" I got up to wash my hands and proceeded to pick my teeth and squeeze two pimples in the mirror.

He echoed from the shower, "I feel like we are married too! Go make me breakfast, woman!"

We giggled and laughed together like lovestruck idiots before Terrance threw a pillow at the bathroom door and moaned for us to shut the fuck up.

Douglas and I just knew beyond a shadow of a doubt our future would be together.

We ordered a pizza upon our return to the barracks. The plan was to relax and watch a movie with his roommate, Terrance, and a few others.

But, while the cat's away, the mice will play. We certainly took full advantage of the empty room while everyone was out gathering their share of the pizza payment and booze. Terrance, who was in charge of collecting the money, accidentally walked in on us during an exceptionally compromised position. "Dude, you guys are fucking already? How rude; I was fucking talking to you man... put your dick away for two seconds so I can get your half of the pizza money."

Douglas passed him the money with his pants half down then resumed kissing me. Terrance left the room, mumbling audibly. "You guys do what you do, but the fucking pizza will be here in forty-five minutes."

I stopped Douglas in the middle of things to tell him that I needed to use the restroom and rushed myself down the hall. This was going somewhere, but my vagina didn't know it. I enjoyed the kissing, but nothing happened in my pants, and I was embarrassed. The things that should have happened just didn't happen, again, so I did the only thing I could think of to bring moisture to myself... While in the bathroom I stood in a stall with my pants half down quietly listening for anyone. When it was clear it took me less than a minute to masturbate then I zipped my jeans up and walked back to his room. This was my ritual with Franklin so I knew how long it would take for my body to produce wetness after a clitoral orgasm. This guy was amazing, and I didn't want him to think I wasn't interested, nor did I want to attempt sex with my desert vagina. Any woman knows how uncomfortable that is, even with the best of partners. The results of my clever trick were noted by Douglas moments before we had sex as I swung from the hanger pole inside of the wall locker. This fact is unimportant though when you consider the many other events that lead a couple to fall in love.

Who can explain why you fall for someone or what exactly happens? It's all so intertwined with a series of things that lead you to that point. Some people are lucky enough to know when they first realized it was love and can tell a wonderful story to their families or friends. People want to hear about the moment true love engulfed them. Alas, I can't remember anything but just knowing that this person was the one I was meant to be with.

What I can tell you is that I wanted to die when I accidentally slipped the words "I love you" after another sexual encounter where my vagina didn't work. I really thought he would never call me again especially when he didn't say anything in return. I can tell you the story of his "wooing" me under the moonlit sky on the range in Arizona with words in Italian: *Your eyes shine as beautiful as you under the light of the moon.* I can tell you how we were attached at the hip after that night in the club and how natural it was to tell my first love that I just couldn't marry him on the phone. But explaining the "story of the moment it happened" eludes me. I just loved him from the moment I met him no matter what my vagina had to say about it.

Maybe it was when Douglas and I painted my barracks room together, and I received a call from my first love. Almost callously, I broke off our engagement. I don't believe I even cried during the shocking four-minute breakup. Douglas was a little surprised considering my history with Robert. He graciously asked if I needed some time and let me know that if I needed him to leave, he respectfully would. I stared at the floor as I responded, but it wasn't out of guilt. I stared because there was a lack of feeling for a person that I had loved for so long. "Strangely, I'm ok," I said. "I can't believe I just told the love of my life that I cannot marry him, and I am ok." I smiled with charm and poise even though my face was freshly painted from several playful smears of paint from Doug's brush.

By the end of the night the room was mauve but looked more like pink, I was single but looked more like taken, and my lesbian life was present but looked more like breeder beginnings.

Chapter 7

Enchanted is a word you can use to describe a portion of what you feel when you fall in love. All other life ceases to exist when a person is enchanted by the mystical powers of the big L. I can't say that you even know that it is love until you are six feet under it and are unable to breathe without that person.

Douglas and I didn't need a discussion of a future together to know where we were headed. Our conversations consisted of matter-of-fact statements like "when we get married" or "I'm so glad you don't want kids." We honestly have no proposal story either. I was nineteen, he was twenty-three, and it was six weeks later when we drove to get our marriage license. It was more romantic because there was no romance, if that makes any sense. We were in an enchanted whirlwind of the engulfment of love. Oh, someone should chime a triangle and sprinkle fairy dust across this page, it was so heavenly.

The car ride to apply for our marriage license became a last minute confessional as Douglas asked me to pull over. I did without too much question. He was highly agitated so for a while I just assumed that he was nervous. "I have something to tell you," he said. Strangely enough, his request didn't faze me. I'm not sure why but I know that whatever he was about to tell me, no matter how bad it was; wasn't going to change my decision to marry him. So, I entertained his request for my undivided attention by positioning my ass closer to the driver's door and twisting myself in his direction. Patiently, I waited for him to begin with a crooked smile on my face.

When he spoke, his voice cracked like he was tired. He hung his head low although he maintained eye contact. "You might not want to do this with me after what I tell you." He looked down to his hands that were fidgeting with a string on his pants and took a huge breath then exhaled. He lifted his head to the ceiling of the car, took another deep breath as his eyes reconnected to mine. It was as if he was asking the Lord to help him through this. I was patient.

After he exhaled the second time, he practically spit it all out in one long monologue. "Before I met you, I was at a party, and this girl begged me to take her in the back on the balcony. I didn't really want to, but she kind of pulled down my pants and started sucking me off and, you know, I wasn't going to stop her but I really, honestly, didn't like her, but I was drunk but…" Douglas put his hands over his face, laughing in frustration while breathing through his fingers. He sighed and tried to get a grip, but his face was changing colors as his eyes went from tears to fright with wide open clarity. He looked at me in a last ditch effort to gather all his strength and finally released. "She called yesterday and told me she is pregnant. She wants me to help pay for an abortion or start doing paperwork for child support." Douglas stopped, held his breath and sat in an awkward heart-pounding silence.

Calmly I asked him. "That's it?"

"That's it," he said and began inhaling again.

I didn't mean to sound as if I was mocking him, but I was genuinely curious. "Is she about five foot five with short brown hair and huge boobs? Lives in the barracks across the street from you right?" I smiled confidently because I knew exactly what was going on.

Maybe confusion isn't the right word for how he expressed what he was feeling in his facial movements. It was confusion for sure, but it was also that look of *how the fuck does she know*. Much like the face of a skeptic being told his darkest desires by a stranger who claims to be a psychic. He was further dumbfounded by my inability to hold a straight face as I burst into laughter. His puzzlement turned into an uncomfortable sort of relief.

"That hoe," I said and dismissed the whole thing with a hand gesture you would use to wave away a peasant field worker. "That is some funny shit."

"I can't believe you are laughing." He didn't move other than to slowly spread a nervous smile over his face.

"I can't believe you believe that hoe! Listen, the last guy I was fucking before I met you came to me crying with the same story. He told me she said it was either his or Mike's baby. Mike is the other guy I used to doink! This skank is leaving me with all the sloppy seconds. Jesus, this chick is not pregnant. I think it's a scam to get money. Don't give her shit until you see a paternity test. If I was scamming, I would say it was you too because you are the most responsible and respectable one of the three. Fuck that hoe; you aren't having any babies." Again, I dismissed the whole situation with a wave of my hand which gave his tense body unspoken permission to relax. He glared out of the front window to the Arizona Mountains that surrounded the post in quiet relief.

"Okay. You are right," he agreed then looked over to me in the driver's seat still smirking. "Fuck that hoe. Let's go get our license." He was amped that I took things so well, but I cut his excitement short to stop him from leaning over to kiss me. "Wait. Since we are sharing…"

Douglas really thought he had thrown the worst at me, but he wasn't prepared to receive. I figured that since we were in a moment of elation and human redemption, I would go ahead and say what I had to say. I pushed through the heat that was filling my body. My eyes changed, and I was scared.

"You know I'm bi, right? I won't give up women so if you can't handle that maybe we shouldn't get married." My eyebrows lifted to the top of my forehead in a very straightforward manner. I could feel the sweat in my armpits making the skin slide around when I moved. He was slightly surprised at my retort but what he didn't know was that this was a side note compared to the secret yet unveiled. I knew my sexuality was not an issue for Douglas but being open and honest about it while ten minutes from the courthouse was serious business. It was like – I love you but here is this thing that you must accept or I'm not driving another two feet. I needed to make sure this issue was crystal clear, so I repeated it. "I won't give up women." The Arizona sun burned through the glass onto my left arm as the air conditioner blasted cold air on my right. The sweat remained, but he was accepting of it and joked about working something out. As if that wasn't a huge issue, I figured I would hit him with another honest zinger just to make sure he understood what he was getting in to. I tried to just say it and not pause. I figured from my personal history of expression that saying things without thought was a good route. It's like ripping off a band aid because everyone knows that's the best way to remove it. So, I tried to make it quick. If I actually thought about what was coming out of my mouth, I was afraid I wouldn't say it at all.

"Before I met you, I was with this asshole who gave me a V.D. but it is gone now, and I'm finishing up my meds. You would have gotten it by now if I was still infected." I shied away, covering my mouth with my hand looking at him with widened eyes. I choked on my spit a little as I stopped breathing for a moment to let him digest the information. The sun burned at my arm. He scrunched his eyebrows together.

"What do you have?" His voice trailed upward in pitch.

"No, I don't have it anymore. It was genital warts," I corrected him with my hands still over my mouth.

"That's forever!" He was surprisingly calm having just heard his fiancé, to whom he was about to commit himself, admitting to having had a venereal disease.

"No, herpes is forever. I had genital warts. They are gone now. I swear it." I corrected him for a second time with the shield of fingers loosely crossed over my lips.

"It's gone?" His demeanor was inquisitive rather than judgmental.

"It's gone," My voice was quiet as I finally dropped my hands into my lap but maintained eye contact as if my life depended on it. He knew as I did that purging was probably the best thing we could have done before finalizing paperwork.

"Pinky swear it?" he held his hand up, pinky finger extended. I looked to his previously broken pinky that never quite healed right then to his big brown eyes. The air was clear and clean, so I shook my head, grabbed his crooked finger with mine and giggled. "Anything else?" he added with a firm squeeze around my little finger.

"I got nothin'. That's it. Clean slate now. You?"

"Nope, I'm good. Skeletons are all out. Let's get married, ya dirty barracks hoe." He laughed a fantastic pure, wholehearted laugh as I put the car in gear and looked for traffic. The left turning signal ticked through my surprise.

"You got jokes! Ok, when your bastard son comes knocking on our door for a child support check, we'll see who was the barracks hoe. Go ahead, tell your bastard son you da baby daddy."

"Ohhhhh burn! That's a good one coming from a cum-guzzling gutter slut. Boo-yeah puta!"

The jokes went on like that getting more vulgar at each stop light until we had to whisper them in each other's ear while we stood in line at the courthouse. It must have looked as if we were in an enchanted whirlwind of love.

I didn't talk much about Doug and the whirlwind of young love to my family. My sister knew more about him than anyone but never figured I would run off to get married. I told my mother what my plans were the week before we were to elope in Vegas in a slip up on the phone. She was so hurt and caught off guard that she and her second husband immediately drove from Ohio to Arizona to meet this punk kid. I'm sure their plan was to deter me from a horrible fleeting mistake. A mother's idea of her daughter's wedding does not involve jeans, or an ordained minister dressed as Elvis. This is why her eyes were swollen with tears when she finally arrived in the small western town outside of the military installation. You could tell she had her husband stop at a gas station so she could splash a little water on her saddened face and attempted to hide red eyes with makeup.

Doug and I met Mom and her second husband at a local award-winning steak house that was a brothel until the Gold Rush ended. We used the history of the place to strike up ice-breaking conversation. It worked, and they both seemed a little calmer by the end of dinner. None of which made it any easier to not be a part of the wedding. The truly sad part was that we left for Las Vegas right after the meal was finished. We had no idea she was coming until she called that afternoon to let me know she was a few hours away.

Mom drove across the United States of America to rescue her daughter from insanity; after dinner, she watched me drive off to the city of sin. I broke my mother's heart, but for some reason, her only verbal protest consisted of one question, "Are you sure?"

If there was more, I didn't hear it. In fact, I was so self-absorbed that when I opened the box of gifts my mother had selected in haste, I passed judgment on almost every item. I was ashamed that she went to the thrift store, embarrassed that she spent money she didn't have on items I didn't want. I was reluctant to take joy in her attempt to salvage her dreams for my wedding day. I pitied her and thought it was cute how she tried to make it special for me.

My egotistical mind was arrogant to what I was doing to everyone but myself and my new fiancé. I thought I was being humble in my desire to be in love. I didn't need a frilly dress and huge ceremony to feel that or proclaim it. Weddings are for families and friends anyway. It was as true to me then, as it is now; only I can say it with older wiser convictions.

Weddings *are* for friends. They want to see your happiness at a ceremony and cry with you as they have done with every major event shared between friends. They *are* for family. Siblings want to be a part of supporting who you vow to spend the rest of your life with and witness the passion to which you devote yourself to another person. Mothers want to be in the back and do whatever it is they do to comfort their daughters and cry uncontrollably as the vows are said. Fathers want to give their daughters away and share that special "father and daughter" dance before another man becomes the center of her world. It's a religious experience. It's tradition. It's the right way to declare that two people are one in the eyes of friends, family, the legal system, and God. I was just fucking ignorant enough to think that I could be in love without the approval of anyone.

Doug and I drove to Las Vegas in his immaculate black car with the marriage license stowed away in a book bag he carried throughout high school. Mom's box of white wedding gifts sat opened in the back seat minus the tiara that read: *I'm the bride*. That was on my head until the cheap plastic dug into the back of my ears about fifteen minutes into the drive.

Sometime during hour number three after the singing and frantic chatting died down slow music and the hypnotizing road gave pause for reflection. "This is just crazy."

"Isn't it?" I agreed. "What are you going to say to your parents? They are going to hate me." I immediately looked beyond the farthest mountain of the Arizona desert as it slowly seemed to move with our travel.

"No, they won't. Did you tell your dad yet?"

I whipped my head to him and shot daggers from my eyes. Doug knew my dad, and I had a falling out just before I turned 18. Three weeks before my birthday, I moved in with my mother and didn't talk to him for almost a year until I went home for Sunny's wedding. Since then, I had discovered independence, sexuality, the value of a dollar, and my right to utterly break free from a living Diablo I knew as my step-mom. Thus, creating an insurgency against my father and anything else that I felt was holding back my life force.

"No, I did not. He is seriously going to kill me." I looked to the mountains again for comfort.

"You should call him."

"I will once we get there," I assured him as a beautiful bird gracefully dove to the earth and lifted in its grasp a small desert snake.

My dad was unfairly oblivious to the happenings in my life as I met and surprised my future in-laws with the news. I'm sure they thought I was a lovely foolish girl, but nothing topped the insanity of calling my dad. I'd never mentioned a word about Doug to him. He didn't even know I was seeing someone else other than Robert back home. In fact, my dad was still building a son-in-law relationship with my first love when I decided to tell him the news.

When we finally arrived in Las Vegas, and all of the hugs had gone to each one of his family members I called my dad. "Guess where I'm at." I paused for a moment as Douglas sat with me on the bed.

He was relaxed and calm. "I don't know, where?"

"Las Vegas!"

"You are? What are you doing there?"

"I'm getting married tomorrow. Do you want to talk to your future son-in-law?" I said all in one fell swoop. It was so easy for me to smile and say it without shaking or worry because the clarity of the decision to be married was so obvious. I knew I was hurting feelings and crushing parental dreams, but I never once second guessed myself. And believe me, I am typically the queen of constant reassurance. It was pure self-centered bliss with Doug, and anything outside of my protective box meant nothing, even breaking my father's heart.

"WHAT!" he yelled, outraged. "No, I don't want to talk to him! Who is this kid? I've never heard you talk about… what's his name? Where did you meet him? What about Robert?"

I attempt to calm him. "Dad. He's 25, about 6'2", 165lbs, dark hair, big brown eyes. His parents are Spanish, German and Italian. They live in Vegas, and we are staying with them right now…"

Dad cuts me off. "Italian. Are they in the mob?" For a second, he thought all of this was a joke and he actually laughed. "You are kidding, right?"

"What? Oh my God, Dad, no." I laughed a bit, thinking he is taking this pretty well. "No Dad, I'm serious. I'm going to marry him tomorrow; we are going to a chapel…"

I heard my dad mumble and then shout something before he threw the phone down. So, there I was, sitting on the bed mouthing the words "he's pissed" to Doug and my future mother-in-law who walked in with her arms crossed with uncertainty.

My sister picked up the phone. With disapproval in her hushed voice, she said, "Janell, what did you say to him? He is pissed, and I think he is crying."

"I'm in Las Vegas, and I'm getting married tomorrow," I announced without hesitation.

"You are not! Are you kidding me? This is not funny. He is in the other room in tears, and Robert lost twenty pounds since you broke off the engagement. What are you doing?" She quietly yelled at me.

"He did?" I murmured.

"This is not funny. I don't even want to talk to you right now." I could hear her give the phone to my step-mother.

"Janell," She drew out my name in a way that neither calmed nor scolded me. She used a pale, smooth voice and very slowly said, "Your dad is very upset. I don't know what's going on or what you said; I have never seen him like this, but I'm going to hang up now."

I could tell she pushed the button on the phone to quietly end the call in eerie silence rather than the familiar clicking sound when you just put the receiver down. I looked to Doug who was staring at me with eyes bigger than a Precious Moments figurine.

"Oh my God. He is crying." I told him.

Doug translated the events to his mother in Spanish. She teared up a bit with loving, understanding eyes and in broken English, said, "I understand. It's too mush mejo. Too mush." She shook her head and cried while explaining a few things in Spanish. I didn't need to understand the words to get that we were not just building our dreams; we were killing theirs.

Despite confusion and reservation Doug's family slap-dashed themselves into appropriate attire for an impromptu Vegas wedding. We traveled from chapel to chapel trying to find one that was open. Unfortunately, it was around the Thanksgiving holiday and even in the city of sin, locals' closed shop early to spend time with their families.

Doug, in the backseat with me, became sullen as sweat oozed from each of his pores. Every chapel was met with disappointment from the neon "closed" signs in the windows. Between stops the traffic was nearly halted to a complete stop, prolonging our disastrous attempt to be married.

After the first hour of chapel hunting, Doug began to smell so bad that we had to open the windows for fresh air. The sweat soaked through his clothing and his face seemed to be an unnatural hue of green. "Are you okay honey? You're not talking much." I asked as I patted his forehead with the back of my hand.

"I'm okay," he said with a forced smile. "I just don't feel well. Maybe it's nerves."

"Well, you smell like ass. Do you want to go home?"

"I'm sorry, but no, I'm okay. Let's get married." He gathered all of his energy to push himself out of the slumped position he was in against the door. He was humble to pretend it was nothing but a case of bad nerves.

A half hour and three closed chapels later Doug was not laughing at any jokes and smelled like a hot landfill under the Georgia sun. By this point, the family was becoming fixated on locating any open chapel on the strip.

From the back seat, I requested to go back home because it was obvious Douglas state of health was in jeopardy. "We should stop. Everything is closed, and Doug is really sick. We can always come back."

Rico, my future brother-in-law, turned from the driver's seat, his butt-chin protruding in Doug's general direction. "Maybe this is an omen telling you not to marry this dumb-leva!"

Doug's mother scolded him for not paying attention to the road before they spoke in Spanish. Suddenly Rico was turning onto a side street headed home, and I was smirking quietly in the back at my future mother in laws ability to control her adult children with a few words. By the time we arrived, Doug was moaning horribly and smelled of sewer sludge. We helped him up the stairs where he succumbed to vomiting and diarrhea from suspected food poisoning. Before going to bed, Doug asked me if I thought this really is an omen.

"No," I tell him. "This just means you are a jack ass for eating rotten yams. Now go to sleep because you smell so fucking bad. I love you."

In the week following our adventure to Las Vegas, I discussed my desperation for a place to marry with a co-worker. A friend who received his judgeship was already in order to make it official. We did not choose the day of our marriage; it was a process of elimination that boiled down to availability of the judge, witnesses, and location.

For us, nothing was as important as the marriage itself. I remember Doug's concern was real and genuine when he asked if ditching the traditions was what I really wanted to do on our return from Las Vegas. "Do you want to get married in a church?"

"For what? We're not religious, so I think it would be hypocritical."

"What about a dress and flowers?" He dug further to verify my wishes.

"Honey, you know I don't give a shit about some dress. I don't care if we get married in jeans."

"Are you sure? Because you know I could care less about all that traditional crap. That's a woman thing anyway, but if you want it, I will make it happen."

"I honestly swear to you that I don't want it." I placed my hand on his leg as he drove, to assure him that the words coming out of my mouth were the truth.

With sincerity and intention, he proclaimed, "I'll get you a ring in a few months, I promise."

"Seriously, I don't want a ring either." Immediately I corrected him. "A ring means nothing to me, and really, I think we should spend our money on things that we need."

He reiterated, "So no ring, no church, no dress?" as he held up a finger to each item.

"Right. And my judge friend will perform the ceremony for free. God, I'm the best fiancé on the planet! No wonder you love me."

"The most important thing is getting married, not how or where it's done," he replied.

This truly was the case because when Jason, the newly ordained judge, arrived at the house, he was in a terrible hurry to coach his son's baseball game. If something were more important to us than getting married, we would have never let Jason walk into that house in full uniform to include cleats under his black judge's robe.

Doug's roommate, two of my coworkers, and the homeowners with whom I had met ten minutes prior to the ceremony were witnesses. Judge Jason rolled up to the address with his window rolled down, "You want to get married in a house? Well, I hate to rush things, but I have my son's game to coach, and I am running so late, so I hope you don't mind if we hurry this up a bit; God I am sweating, my air conditioner broke yesterday." He walked, and as he did the cleats, he wore clicked against the cement.

"Well, *this* must be the lucky man!" Jason extended his hand to Doug for a hearty handshake.

Douglas tried to introduce himself and give thanks for doing this on such a short notice, but Jason was rushing him into the house with a hand on the middle of his back. "Listen, let's go inside. Do they have a room so we can do a little private counseling before we start?" His eyes darted back and forth between us. Just then the homeowners opened the door to their home. My friend who organized the whole thing, pushed through the homeowners to give me a hug and shake Doug's hand. Meanwhile, Jason introduced himself to everyone else as Doug whispered hard, "He has fucking cleats on. Did you see that?" Then he laughed so loud I had to rub the ringing in my ear out. Once we were in the door, we immediately noticed artwork that we both found horrendous. Doug whispered again, "Dude, they have a velvet pug picture on the fucking wall."

I nudged him hard, "You realize you aren't whispering anymore!"

We gathered eight adults in a very small living room, each of us involved in deep, separate thoughts. The homeowners were sort of pushed into the adjacent dining room area. They probably couldn't believe they'd said yes to this. The wife was obliviously staring at Jason's shoes. Doug's roommate was excited but somewhat indifferent. He just wanted to know about the after party as he stood with crossed arms next to the wall with the velvet pug. My coworkers stood in uniform next to each other with smiles from ear to ear. They'd recently begun an affair that hadn't quite turned sexual, or maybe it had? They too thought, "These white folks are crazy!"

Douglas and I held hands. Our hearts and minds felt the same love. Then there was Jason, frantic with the preoccupation of his son's game. "So, come on, come on, come on in here guys… you don't mind if we use your bedroom for a minute, do you?" The hosting couple reluctantly waved us in. Hell, why not?

We sat on their bed as Jason knelt next to us. He pulled out folded papers and a pen from his robe pocket, flattening them as best as he could onto his robe then the mattress. "Okay, you are Douglas," he muttered, scribbling it over a name already crossed out. "Do you prefer Doug or Douglas?"

"Either one," He answered.

"Are you guys religious?"

"No. You can take out the God stuff," I said.

Jason mumbled some of the text and crossed out three paragraphs. He flipped a few pages and marked through a whole page. "Shit, that got rid of a lot! This is my first-time guys, hang tight. So, I'm going to say, 'Do you Doug take Janell blah bibbity blah and when I say 'With this ring'... Do you have the rings?"

"We don't."

Jason entered into a whole other state of panic, "What do you mean?" He looked to Doug for his answer. "Like, you don't have them now?"

"No," I had to put his mind at ease. "We don't need rings to symbolize our love."

Jason instantaneously rushed through his pages again and removed additional paragraphs. The sweat was dripping down his left temple, but no one told him, and he didn't bother to wipe it away. "Well guys, this is great; I have less than a page to read. It's going to be like, do you... do you... talk a little bit about unity and love then kissy-kissy, sign the papers and I'm out. I got to get to the game. Do you have any questions?"

"I'm good. Let's get hitched," We practically declared in unison.

We walked out and stood near the velvet pug picture as Jason read his one-page ceremony. We cried, did the kissy-kissy, and signed the papers just as instructed. After thanking the homeowners, we left to eat at a restaurant we couldn't afford and ended up going to sleep around ten thirty that night on a twin bed in the barracks. We reminisced over our attempts to be married in Las Vegas, the cleats and velvet pugs.

"That would be a good book," Doug remarked, "About how you dissed me at the club, dumped your ex, the whole Vegas food poisoning thing—which is an omen I just ignored by the way and now the judge with the baseball uniform under his robe. I'm going to tell my grandkid, hey little Johnny; I remember my beautiful wedding to your grandma back in 1997. See the photos with the velvet pug? We had our honeymoon on a twin bed in the barracks." He laughed and snuggled closer to me.

I replied with a yawn and hiccup from one too many Long Island iced teas with my steak. "Well, I think it's a FAN-fucking-TASTIC story, but I'm totally falling to sleep."

"What about honeymoon sex?" Doug slurred most of his words.

"Tomorrow, honey. We can tomorrow." I mumbled as I awkwardly tapped his thigh.

"Okay good because I think my soldier's unable to… the position of attention…" He lifted the blankets and yelled in the darkness. "A-ten-CHUN! Medic! Nope, see, he's dead."

I hiccupped again and laughed. God, I loved my husband.

Chapter 8

The next step was to begin sharing a life together and build a unity between two people. We became ecstatic over little pleasures like picking out dishes and shower curtains. We held hands as we said yes to the loan for our cherry wood bedroom set, leather couch, and Lhasa Apso we lovingly named Bean.

Accepting our stance as a future yuppie couple included items purchased beyond our means and eating new and healthy foods. We played the latest music, had a new car, and never wore old clothes. All of which set the standard for where we wanted to be in twenty years.

They say the things you do reflect where you are in your life. For instance, if you do a massive cleaning of your closet and donate all the crap you don't use, it means you are starting over or beginning a new chapter. Out with the old, in with the new! If you look in your wardrobe and realize that the once vibrant, gemstone items have all gone to earth tones you have either found security and settled or seek a change.

If everything one does is reflective of one's life, it is clear that I was in a fresh, positive start to a long-term relationship. Let's analyze the symbolism, shall we? Cherry wood is hard, uncommon, and has a fine, polished look. Leather is durable, yet flexible. A new puppy takes patience, nurturing, and communication. All descriptions are worthy of comparison to my life, my outlook, and my relationship.

I was happy, content, and every other wonderful word to describe utopia. We had everything we needed and began to live as one, eventually settling into a groove of our own. Morning routines were well-choreographed dances in and out of the bathroom, timed with designated days for walking the dog. I fell more and more in love with him every time he made the bed or brought home a house plant because he knew that I had a green thumb. I loved the quick, playful squeezes as we passed each other to do mundane household chores. My infamous finger up his ass move was perfected for just the right high pitched yelp that always threw me into hysterics.

Expendable dog children aside, I never wanted kids. As far as I can remember this fact holds true even when at fourteen, my step-mom predicted that I would be barefoot and pregnant in my trailer by the time my twenty-second birthday arrived. This was part of dinner conversation that my family shirked off as a joke until the prediction for my sister was a successful businesswoman, unmarried in a new home with a new car in the driveway. But I digress.

I probably informed Doug of this long-standing opinion on our way to get our marriage license, somewhere in between his possible bastard son confession and my genital warts admittance. He was just tickled pink over this news. One of the many reasons he married me, I'm sure.

So, it was a shock to him when, early into our marriage, I begged almost daily to start a family.

At lunchtime, we traditionally met at our apartment. One afternoon, my emotions got the best of me, and I decided I wanted to have kids. He walked in the door to find me crying on the couch with Bean, our Lhasa Aphso, balled comfortably on my lap. "What are you blubbering about?" He walked past me toward the kitchen.

"We should have a baby, Doug. No! We should adopt!" I smeared tears on the sleeve of my military uniform.

He laughed and looked to the T.V. to see the station dedicated to women's issues, stories, and, as Doug would call it, the period-hormonal, I'm not a sex object bullshit whiney channel. "Oh God, are you watching the adoption show again? He said as he opened a can of soup and put it in the microwave. He walked into the living room to stand between me and the television as he waited for his lunch to cook.

I shook my head yes and wiped heartbreaking tears from my face again with the sleeve of my uniform. "I can't help it. There are so many kids out there... we would make good parents."

"We are good parents, aren't we, Bean?" Doug said in his best voice as he ruffled the top of the dog's head. Bean backed away from him in my lap with her ears down and peed on my uniform. "We have plenty of time for that Janell. Anyway, whatever happened to you *not ever* wanting kids?" He returned to the kitchen to stir his food.

"Throw me a towel. I don't know; I changed my mind," I said.

"You need to stop watching that tampon channel. It's infectious. Next, you'll bedazzle the couch and decoupage my fish tank!" He threw the towel across the room, and it smacked me in the face, but his comments were lighthearted, and he was giggling. The dog, however, was irritated when I scooted her out of the way to soak up the piss on my leg.

"You are an insensitive cock head," I pouted as I wiped and patted my lap.

"And you is a whiney*ha-o*!" He smiled and blew on his hot soup to cool it down.

"A what?"

He smiled gladly willing to repeat it. "A *ha-o*!" Doug rolled his neck for additional giggles.

"A ho? Are you trying to be ghetto?" It was comical to hear him say any word in slang since his vocabulary was extensive and his mindset could be considered on the brink of scholarly.

"Yeah nigga," he said as he placed a hand over his balls with a face reminiscent of *An American Pimp* after the character told his hoe to "Bring me my money, bitch!"

"Oh, *lord*! You are right; I don't want kids with you; they will come out retarded, and I'll have to walk them to the short bus that you will be driving."

"You know you *luuuuv* me." His head rolled again as he shoveled another two scoops of soup into his mouth in a hurry to get back to work.

"I don't love you."

He drank the last of it from the bowl and with food still in his mouth he said, "You just love my doggie style." Doug laughed as he rinsed the bowl out and placed it into the dishwasher perfectly aligned and spaced evenly from the other dirty ones.

"What size helmet do you wear?" I said with "smartass" written all over my face.

"What? I can't hear what you're saying with my cock in your mouth." His high pitched laugh began a familiar techno beat as he walked over to me, Bean, and the piss soaked towel.

"Fucker." It was all I could manage to come back with as I sniffed the last of the snot from my nose.

"Puta la gata," he said as he gently cradled my head with his hand to bring it forward. He gave me a loving kiss on my forehead and lingered in that position for a second before he stepped away. "I love you. I've got to go."

Bean climbed into her comfortable curled position on my lap, lifted her jowls, exposed teeth, and timidly growled. Doug pointed his finger right in her face making the dog flinch. "*You... are expendable.*"

After our names came up on the list to obtain on-post housing, we moved from our cozy apartment to a place inside the military installation. At the time, government housing in Arizona was lacking in aesthetics, to say the least. Curb appeal was nonexistent.

Our backyard, which was supposed to be lush green grass according to post regulations, was regular dry desert dirt. It was hard and packed down. Only a few yellow patches of grass managed to sprout through, if weeds native to Arizona hadn't taken over already. Nevertheless, Doug and I took great pains to keep it free of debris and water it often after hand-tossing grass seeds in an attempt to grow our own oasis. We took turns holding the hose to spray our seedlings as the other raked dog shit from the Labrador and German Shepherd we adopted.

Bean was in a better home by this time since Doug's ultimatum was, "It's me or the dog." Poor Bean had to go. Our new dogs could have cared less if grass was there or not. As long as we raked, they were happy to crap on clean ground. But we tried, Lord knows we did.

As the realization of wasted effort began to set in, we inevitably just threw the hose off of the back patio and let the water run down to pool in the yard. Surely the grass would drink, and we would be the envy of our neighbors.

One late afternoon in the midst of our ritualistic attempts at landscaping, a neighbor walked from her driveway to our back gate to say hello. She carefully held the hand of a three-year-old child as her silky brown ponytail swayed across her back. Her cheeks were thick and pink when she smiled to introduce herself. "Doncha love the grass here? Hi, I am Kay. My husband and I see ya'll workin' so hard to fix it but believe me it just blows away in the desert. This is my daughter Ellie."

There was just something warm and welcoming about Kay and her big brown eyes. She was refreshingly honest and open right from the beginning. It's unexplainable really, but the connection was very sisterly and genuine. Our entire conversation was instant bonding on every level.

After talking a while, we became so comfortable with each other the skeletons simply ran out of the closet! Her daughter was a product of her first marriage in which she had an affair after she found out that he gave her a venereal disease. Kay told me that she really did not know if the baby was that of her ex-husband or the other man.

"The doctors told me that because of the scarring I may not be able to carry a pregnancy to full term, so girl, I freaked and tried for six months before she came. But Tim doesn't know this, and I think he would break down if I told him all of it," she confessed. Then just as quickly as she told me her secrets, she changed the subject completely. "Oh, ya'll should come over for supper tomorrow. I'll make brisket."

The meet and greet was quick, fierce and well received for both couples. The next evening, we shared a meal of Texas-style mashed potatoes, brisket with various vegetables and spices, and a dessert to die for with beer for the boys. I'd say that was some good old fashioned entertainment.

Doug and I laughed all evening and shared stories with Kay and Tim as if we had known them for years. I helped Kay clean up the table as Tim and Doug discussed "man stuff" that we were not privy to as they tossed toys for the dogs. It was absolutely wonderful to meet friends who were just like us, young, happily married, and all around good people. When the night finally closed in, Doug and I walked through our shit-free dirt backyard hand in hand.

Over the next week, our nightly watering became a running joke between the four of us. By the following week when they came over for our dinner invite, the only life that had grown was a grass patch in the spot where Doug and I stood to water the dirt. Apparently, our leaking nozzle gave the extra nourishment it needed to grow. Tim and Kay took great care to jump over our precious green patch before knocking at our sliding glass door, alcohol in hand. Once again dinner was more of the same happy atmosphere and when it was over the boys were told to do the dishes this time while the ladies freshened up for our night out.

Kay was plain and very forgettable if it wasn't for her fantastic smile that produced dimples, emphasizing her vivacious personality. She was not in the best shape, but she was by no means fat. Her body would have toned up nicely if she had time away from being a full-time mother to do a few sit-ups every now and then. Kay was a typical cute mom, the kind that dotes over her husband at every military barbecue and volunteers at the county fair painting kids' faces for free. But this description makes her seem almost dowdy, homely, or like a jolly fat lady in a moo-moo. Kay is not to be associated with a woman who wears a tent and calls it a dress, no sir. She dressed very well when the occasion called for it, and that night her hair was down and styled to look rich and silky like fine chocolate, unlike the frayed ponytail I had seen her wear all week. Her eyes were framed with a little brown eyeliner and mascara which brightened her almond color. Kay wore the most daring red lipstick, which looked a little sleazy but somehow sexy at the same time. Her jeans fit every curve, and her top peeked open at the chest to reveal a black lace bra if she tilted just right.

"My daughter painted my nails this color, girl. I didn't have time to take it off so I just found this lipstick and slapped it on so it would match. Is it too much? Do I look like a hooker?" She laughed and didn't give me time to answer. "Well ya'll," she said into the mirror. "I'm not a housewife tonight!" Kay gave her reflection a kiss before we opened the door to the bathroom, walked through the hairspray cloud, down the hallway to the kitchen. Doug and Tim finished their cleaning duties and held prepared drinks for us as we pranced toward them.

"Ta-da!" Kay shouted as the boys whistled. "What were ya'll talkin' about while we were putting our faces on?" She pulled out a bar stool and sat on it. I followed suit.

"That we are the luckiest men on this earth with hot wives," Tim said as he handed drinks out to each of us.

We were swooned by this gesture of our suave men. As we took our first sip Doug chimed in, "And how you are all getting fucked in the butt tonight." The guys burst into red-faced laughter as they leaned on each other for support and slapped the countertop. Kay and I heaved forward in an attempt to keep the fluid from bursting out of our mouths, but our attempts were futile.

"You assholes!" I wiped the mixed drink from my nose and scurried to the sink. "I almost fucking choked!" I hovered over the sink, letting the booze drip from my nose as I spit and eventually tried to clean off my face without smearing my makeup.

Tim switched into the kind of laughter that some people refer to as the silent tick. Apparently, it's when something is so funny it steals all sound, yet they are able to tick and laugh with their mouths wide open. A tear couldn't have made its way out of his eyes; they were squeezed so tightly. Tim was frozen in this position as his face just deepened in its shade of red. From the quiet pressure of the silent tick, a moist clicking noise squeaked through every time he tried to breathe.

Doug's laugh transformed into a high pitched monotone techno song, producing a steady beat of shrill man noises until, in an effort to breathe, a deep snort interrupted the flow, which threw Tim into hysterics on the floor, silently ticking.

Kay and I scurried around the island, past Tim on the floor and Doug who was wheezing. Our hands tried to catch the liquid still dripping from our noses. We stood at my kitchen sink, towels at our chins while the boys gave each other high fives in a true male-bonding form.

There is something to be said for the innocence of youth. When a person gets older, things like this may get a chuckle at best, but these theatrics makes being twenty a viable reason to build a time machine.

After recomposing ourselves, the four of us had a wonderful night dancing and drinking. We tried to watch a movie after coming back home, but if a wisecrack about anal sex sent us into hysterics, a movie was not the best up-tempo idea. The four of us got bored, and since drinks were low, the boys agreed to a beer run, which made me responsible for entertaining Kay. The first thing I grabbed was my photo album. We flipped through the pages looking at photos of my life before marriage when Melanie, Annica, and Lynn demonstrated the universal lesbian sign in practically every shot. Kay complimented my appearance in each picture, even the random high school photos that fell out of the back of the book. She couldn't stop telling me how pretty or hot I looked and how envious she was of me. She joked that if she was gay, she would sleep with me and we laughed—although she seemed serious and it made me slightly uncomfortable.

When the photo album was out of pages I turned to music and crouched by the stereo to flip through CDs I thought she would like. It definitely helped me to break eye contact yet still be engaging. I played specific songs for her as she swayed in enjoyment. Her compliments continued as did her smiles and gentle touches.

I thought I was picking up faint signals of interest but ignored them all until Kay boldly said, "I'm totally serious. I'd let you fuck me. Hey, maybe we should go to my place. I have CDs you might like." I didn't even have time to think about anything. When she opened the door of opportunity, I walked in it as fast as we walked through my shitty dirt yard to her front door.

When we opened it, we were met with a beautiful blue glow from a huge terrarium that held a snake. We walked over to it as she excitedly explained the species and how terrible she felt for the mice when she had to feed it. She didn't turn on any lights as she walked down the dark hallway into a bedroom. From the room, she called to me, "Come back here! I didn't show you our new bedroom set, did I?" I walked slowly as my eyes adjusted. She was sitting on the corner of the bed smiling as I approached the doorway.

"The light switch is behind you," Kay said.

The bright light made both of us wince when I flipped the switch. She bounced and beamed, "It's so wonderful! Come try it!"

I took two steps into the room and pressed on the mattress with my hands. "Sure is nice," I agreed.

Kay stood up. "Sit. You have to sit on it." She walked to the light switch and flipped it off as I sat on the corner of her new bed.

"Why did you turn the light off?" I asked her silhouette.

"I don't know." She stood staring at me with the blue illumination on one side of her face. I sat for a second and let a feeling swell inside that told me I should do something, but I chickened out. "We should probably go." Kay didn't move she just stood in the doorway as I sat on the bed. To move through the awkward moment, I nervously stood up in the dark and moved my hand as if Vanna White was presenting a vowel. "Well, you lead the way." My brain was swirling like it was trying to solve a riddle. What did this feeling want me to do and why was it pressing to have it accomplished this instant? In slow motion, Kay turned to face the blue light, so I stood to follow. My body and mind screamed in unison for me to make a move. I could almost hear the words as the connection from my head to my mouth wiggled my tongue to do it now, or I would never do it. A slap is the worst that could happen and, even then, I could blame it on the alcohol, so there was nothing to lose.

In an instant that seemed like a lifetime, I grabbed her shoulders, spun her around, and pressed her against the wall for a passionate kiss. At first, she uttered a surprised "Oh" much like an actress in a classic film. Her body was rigid and a little scared. She then relaxed a little to return kisses when her mind wrapped around the idea. When she realized that this was turning her on, she moaned and wrapped her arms around me to pull me in for more. It was a brief two minutes of uninhibited passion before we paused to shake things off.

Her eyes squinted as she licked her lips and let her head roll away from me on the wall for support. What she was saying versus what her body was telling me was two different things altogether. "The boys should be back by now; we should go," Kay whispered as she heaved upward and rolled her body against mine. She grabbed my breasts as she rolled her hips and leaned in for another kiss. She repeated telling me that we needed to leave between kisses and rubbing each other's clit through the seams of our pants. I was the one who stepped away from her in an effort to actually leave the hallway. It took her a second to realize that I wasn't coming back, so she slowly turned to walk toward the door without saying anything. When she reached it, she hesitated opening it. I kissed her once more just to hear her moan again and reminded her that maybe we should bring some CD's back since that's our cover story as to why we left. We giggled.

My eyes were focused on where I was going, unlike Kay who was giggling, smiling and rubbing my arm as we walked in the dark toward the shining light from my living room windows. I felt liberated over what just happened, and I was happy, but she reverted to a girl after her first finger bang. She was hanging on me and very fluid with her movements which was more from arousal than from the alcohol.

"They are going to know. I can't stop smiling." She said as if I didn't notice.

"No, they are not. Just act normal." I gently slid my right hand down my left arm to detach her hold on me.

"I can't. I want to kiss you again." She said after I had separated us.

"Shut up. I do too. Keep walking." I was smiling of course, but I knew that we could not go back into the house smelling of each other while shooting flirtatious glances.

We arrived to the back sliding glass door and opened it to see the boys sitting on the couch drinking beers. Our drinks sat in a pool of condensation while the husbands talked and waited for us to return. Tim asked what took us so long and looked unbelieving as we explained ourselves like guilty children. I hoped the boys didn't see the state of arousal in my face or the way I stood uneasily.

Kay and I sat at the island sipping our drinks and chatting away, hoping a conversation would make the pulse in our loins disappear. Tim and Doug stood in the middle of the living room talking. Every now and then their laughter would burst through the music halting our conversation long enough for a look before we resumed chatting.

During one pause, the husbands seemed to twitch to the music. "Are they trying to break dance?" I asked Kay. She shrugged as we watched their horrible attempts to simulate robotic movements. They tried feverishly to mimic the jerking of eighties break dancing favorites.

"Come on girls," Tim said as he jerked and posed in random awkward positions. "Come (pause and pose) break dance (pause and pose) with us."

"Yeah," Doug shouted with boyish excitement as he tore off his shirt. "Bet you can't beat this move." He spreads his hands out like Jesus on the cross. A movement began in his left hand to his elbow and left shoulder. The flow traveled through his neck over his right shoulder and seemed to shift down his entire right arm until his fingertips finished the wavelike motion where he pointed to Kay who threw her head back in laughter and intense clapping.

Tim, never to be outdone, stripped down to his boxers, sat on the government tiled floor then forced his body to spin like a top on his bony ass. The faster Tim spun, the higher Doug's laughter got. Then he took his pants off to join Tim. Kay asked why the boys are getting naked.

"Because they are idiots," I answered, obviously unimpressed.

"Because we are hot for you, baby," Tim tells his wife. "Come on. Dance with us," he begged as the song changed automatically.

I looked over to Kay who was dancing a little jig on the bar stool next to me. "Come on Janell, don't you want to dance with me?" she asked as she pulled at my arm. My eyebrows scrunched together questioning if she was even remotely aroused from earlier. She seemed altogether unfazed nudging me with her eyes to hit the floor while our half-baked husbands polished tiles with their asses. I sat on my uncomfortable stool shaking my head as I sipped my drink and "tisked" her in true Annica style.

When the laughter stopped, Kay and I looked over to the boys who waited with bated beer breath for that particular moment. They stood completely naked with hands interlocked behind their heads until our eyes met their midpoints, wherein they rocked back and forth forcing their penises to slap the inside of their thighs. When the slapping beat in rhythm all four of us roared in thunderous laughter. Even I had to admit, that was a good one.

These two were seriously some fucking awesome neighbors. Our backyard "picking up dog shit" conversation will be much more interesting now that I have made out with the wife in the foyer and seen the husband's penis slap his inner thigh until it was red.

Funny as it was, in the moment of the whole situation, I was embarrassed for all of them and still turned on from my little tantalizing teases at Kay's house. I just wanted them to stop being stupid even though I was smiling. I could feel the night getting ugly if they didn't. My husband was my soulmate, but his kisses and his touches never left me in the state I was in. I can't quite put my finger on what it did to me emotionally, but I was noticeably rattled and slightly crabby. I remained in my fully clothed prudishness which felt to me like the only level of stability in all the madness. When surrounded by idiocy, silence is golden, so that's what I did. I kept my mouth shut and just turned away to sip on a drink.

With all my adventures and wild side, I sometimes really wonder how I can be so dual-natured. When faced with people doing stupid things or when I hear the mumblings of morons, disgust overwhelms me which renders me silent. In my head, I repeat the phrase "in the company of fools" over and over with a shake of my head. It's a mystery as to where the saying came from so, I can't give credit but thank you, Jesus, for wise words. The phrase has saved me from rabbit punching someone in the throat on several occasions. When confronted with idiots I repeat it and simply breathe. How I didn't apply this to my own insanity, I'll never know. But I certainly had to repeat it in my head that night because I nearly murdered my half-naked husband, neighbor, and his wife on government housing tiles. Can you imagine what I would have told the military police? *Well, I'm sorry officer but they tried to defile me like devil nymphs, and I begged them to stop.* I think not.

In the company of fools. In the company of fools. In the company of fools.

I guess in all the commotion of the loud music, embarrassment, and ass cheeks squeaking painfully on the floor, my silly little meditation helped me to seize the moment. I was bold. I grabbed Kay's arm and dragged her to the master bedroom. I was completely and utterly on autopilot. All other activities ceased to exist. If silence could ring in one's ears, it would have deafened me. I heard nothing.

At first, the husbands watched then it all took a turn, and the wife swapping happened. Everyone was too intoxicated to have an emotional response. We were young, and nobody was thinking about anything. To be honest, Doug and I were indifferent to the whole situation, and we never talked about it nor did we care that it actually happened. Our neighbors moved to Germany weeks later, and we kind of forgot about that night and them until we were stationed in Germany. That's when we realized that we were at least an hour and a half from where they lived and never attempted to contact them. But why would we? Then by coincidence, we literally met them by accident. We were lost, saw what appeared to be their truck in the parking lot of a military complex, guessed what door it belonged to, and knocked. By dumb luck, Kay answered the door. You cannot get any more random than that.

We stood with Kay and Tim in the hallway after catching up as if we used to be respectable can-we-borrow-some-sugar neighbors. The whole wife swapping ordeal was never mentioned. We even made arrangements for me to stay the night the following evening so Kay and I could catch up and do some shopping. We shopped like normal friends minus one little indiscretion in the changing room. We came home on time, cooked dinner and watched some television with the kids. Kay bathed her daughter and new baby girl. Once they were happily tucked into bed and asleep, we chatted online with men about our friendship, which turned into chatting online with horny men who wanted to see us fuck on web camera. We thought it was funny and had more than a few laughs at their expense.

We finally became bored with their nagging requests for a show and decided to call it a late evening. Our eyes were puffy from lack of sleep and squinting from trying to read computer text for an extended period of time. I headed straight for the bottom bunk in her eldest daughter's room and tucked myself in. Kay retired to the bathroom for a shower. Absolutely nothing out of the ordinary.

However, if my life were truly that boring, I wouldn't be writing a book. So as the story goes Kay leaned over me to shake me awake while her daughter slept above us. There was a deep breath of shock as I was suddenly pulled from the beginning of my slumber before I asked, "What happened? What's the matter?" and rubbed my eyes.

"Nothing, I just wanted you to know that I had so much fun today," she whispered as she knelt next to the bed. I could smell the soap on her skin even as I faced the wall.

"Yeah, me too. Damn you scared me; I totally fell asleep." I twisted to face her in case there was more she needed to say, but frankly, I was tired.

"Janell. Kiss me." She leaned in, and I could tell she had brushed her teeth.

I twisted my back tighter as I tried to whisper as loudly as I could without waking her daughter. "What? No." Before I could say any more, she leaned in to kiss me. Her hair was wet, and I was overwhelmed with the smell of shampoo as strands of her dark locks fell onto my face.

She pulled away saying, "Come to the bathroom." As she stood up, she gently tugged at my arm.

"No, your kid is going to wake up. What about Tim? Didn't you say he doesn't want an Arizona repeat?"

"He had to work early. He's gone, we are alone. Come to the bathroom. I want you."

"Kay, I am going to bed. You are fucking nuts." I rolled over to face the wall. "Go to bed Kay," I pulled my arm free and tucked it to my chest.

She grabbed my shoulder and twisted me toward her again, and that's when I realized she was only in a towel. "Please," she begged.

"Goddammit," I said as I flipped the covers off and let her guide me to the bathroom. She dropped the towel the moment we shut the door, and we attacked each other. I may have said how wrong it was out loud moments before we fucked each other right where we stood. And how quick it was. Rather than sex, it felt like a feverish race to see who could finger bang the other first. The experience was lustful even with sensual kisses that tasted like toothpaste and blood from her recent tooth extraction.

Of our rekindled night of passion, it's sad that the taste of dental work is more prominent than what actually happened. But I said it once, and I'll say it again, "It's the before and after we all sit on the edge of our seats for." The climactic part wasn't the sex; it was the ring she gave me the next morning before I drove home. Kay dramatically pulled me into the bedroom and put a plain gold band in my hand and curled my fingers around it.

"I want you to have this. It was my grandmother's, but I want you to have it because I love you and I want you to think of me every time you wear it. It will be like you are mine and I am yours. Our little secret, okay?"

I tried to explain that I couldn't accept such a gift. After she insisted, my hand reluctantly held firm as she slid it on my finger. I left her place feeling extremely awkward on my long journey home.

It was a two-hour drive on the German Autobahn. Plenty of time to think about Kay and the ring she gave me. I glanced at it on my finger, twisted it around with my thumb, tried to shine it against my shirt, and finally took it off for a while. Silver is my passion, so the gold felt wrong to wear.

After tossing it into the cup holder of Doug's immaculate car, the ring scraped from side to side around each curve of the road. It made me feel guilty, so I pushed it back on my finger. How could she possibly love me? The meaning in her words seemed far too profound for a girl she barely knew and slept with twice. Was she a woman obsessed? I cared for her but certainly did not love her. I was in love with my husband.

Rationalizing these things in my mind, I pitied her.

Chapter 9

After arriving home, the ring disappeared into a pocket in my jewelry box. The meaning and special moment was lost forever because feelings for Kay were not shared. My heart belonged to Doug. My marriage and my life continued to be the most wonderful relationship in existence.

My sex life, however, was beginning to be something of a constant compromise. Douglas was bothered by the fact that we only had sex once a week and he became very vocal about it. "This isn't normal. I need more snatch, woman!" Sadly, this was his chief complaint. So, in order to make things right, we joked at the dinner table about it and bartered for quality pussy time.

"I don't know. Why don't you kiss me or *something*, Doug? You can't just say *get naked* and expect me to be turned on ya fucker. Jesus, why don't *you* take my clothes off?" I laughed then shoveled a pile of food into my mouth.

"Listen, woman; you give me twenty minutes. I ain't got time to fuck around with your bras and buckles and shit," He leaned back against his chair and sipped ice water as he referred to my stipulation which came about years earlier after many marathon sex sessions.

My complaint was that it took too long and was actually uncomfortable not to mention painful when he stuck it in without being fully aroused. This in itself was a problem because I didn't get exceptionally wet to begin with. At some point, when he asked for sex, I started tapping my left wrist where a watch would be worn to let him know that the clock was ticking. On more than one occasion I explained that if he couldn't do what he had to in twenty minutes, something was wrong, and my vagina would shrivel up and fall out if he kept pounding away without lubrication. This stipulation worked for Doug. He took it seriously and maintained the lube drawer, which was always well stocked.

Seventy-five percent of our foreplay went quite literally like this:

"Hey, baby. Do you want to do it?"

Then I would say yes or no depending on what was cooking on the stove and if it could cook unattended or not. If the answer was yes, he would say, "Okay baby, get naked." Then I'd tap my wrist, and he would go running for the KY Jelly. He would put a little on me, put a little on himself and shove it in. Battaboom, battabing, intercourse was over, and I could either masturbate to get off or stir my Spanish rice that was probably boiling over.

Since his principal complaint was about the amount of sex we had, we questioned how much sex was considered normal for an average married couple without kids. We couldn't ask our neighbors. They were apparently worse than rabbits in breeding season. And we really didn't want to know how many times the neighbors' fat military housewives sucked their husband's cocks on a weekly basis.

He just wanted more sex from his wife, whom he was in love with; was that too much to ask? It wasn't like he was a beast! Doug was a good looking fellow with big brown eyes, thick Spanish hair that was always well groomed, and had the cutest dimples when he smiled. The thing is, if more sex was the biggest problem we faced as a couple, we were doing pretty good.

At the end of 2000, while watching television, I saw a commercial recruiting soldiers for the Army Soldier Show. The show consisted of selected soldiers placed on temporary duty to entertain troops across the United States, including one overseas assignment.

Soldiers auditioned for a spot in the show and would also be trained as their own technicians and roadies if they made the cut. Some say it's a soldier spin-off of the Bob Hope USO tours he used to do for the troops in Vietnam. The soldier show motto was, "Entertainment for the soldiers, by the soldiers." High school drama club and summer teen theater had nothing on the fifteen minutes of fame that the soldier show offered. It was bigger, more elaborate, required extensive planning, and had a healthy budget.

The tour was eight months long so a person who wanted to do the show would have to get permission from their unit before they could audition. I spoke with Doug about my desire to do the show, and he agreed to support me with my potentially achievable dream. After gathering all of the necessary paperwork, I sent it to the entertainment installation along with a video of a karaoke performance and my letter of release. Two months later I flew to the United States for the official audition.

There were a lot of talented people during the week-long process. One of whom was a girl named Natalia. She had long, straight brown hair, and stood about two inches taller than me with flawless skin. Her choice of clothing was always on the risqué side with small touches of white trash influences that you couldn't quite pinpoint but knew they were there.

We began our friendship over the uncanny similarities of our mothers. We joked about leading parallel lives as our childhood stories continued to practically mirror each other. Natalia and I shared the same adventures with our mothers' inability to get out of the welfare system and out of the bars. I was shocked but mildly surprised to learn that she was the eldest sibling of a sister the same age as mine, whom she too affectionately nicknamed "Bean." Our friendship was instant, to say the least.

Another common ground was our powerful voices and love of the craft. She claimed to have been the lead singer in a punk band and wanted to take it further. We blew the crowd out of the water when we sang our chosen songs. Natalia and I received the same compliments, and both of us made it into the 2001 Army Soldier Show.

Rehearsals were grueling. Seven in the morning to seven at night would have been a luxury. Our hours varied. The sixteen soldiers who made the cut rotated through voice lessons, choreography, set up, costume fittings, and constant changes to the production. Everyone had assigned places to be throughout the day for maximum efficiency. It was the most organized mess of my military career.

The songs chosen for the show were selected for each soldier by vocal range ability and stage presence. They were then assimilated into groups or sections intermingled with dance numbers and comedy to create a 90-minute variety show. It had to have an aesthetic flow and be kid-friendly, entertainment for teenagers, family members, soldiers of all branches, parents, retirees, and veterans. The entertainment branch had big shoes to fill. The directors worked endlessly to give everyone stage time and maintain the integrity of the show, but sometimes numbers were thrown out due to a myriad of reasons. I personally worked hard to memorize a dance routine when the order of songs changed, making it impossible for me to dance and be on stage with a complete costume switch for the next number. Needless to say, this was one of many numbers my name was cut from.

Everyone was affected by the constant rearrangements. The wardrobe lady, Miss Sue, purchased material and worked nights to make eleven shirts that were worn twice during rehearsals and thrown out. The directors never told us why, but Miss Sue bluntly explained, "You American girls have big hips and flabby arms! Director Vic say you arms too fat in shirt and he say we no have money to buy girdles." Miss Sue pointed to me and continued, "And why you get that tattoo on your arm? You tattoo is like, POW, look at me... I'm a tattoo on arm. And you little! How you have big hips when you look like chopsticks?" Traditional Japanese ballads played on a crappy little cassette player she had set within a nook by the sewing machine.

I was utterly shocked at her candor because I had never heard her say much before, let alone cut us down. "Dang Miss Sue, that is so bold," I said as she moved me out of the way so another thicker girl could be measured and pinned.

"Well, Miss Sue no have fat arms to hide." She tugged at the soldier's shirt. She stopped to look up with a pin hanging from her mouth. "You no eat today. You give it to Chopsticks over there, okay?" The girl's mouth hit the floor as mine did, but we didn't say anything.

Everyone adapted to change, even Miss Sue with much dismay. Eventually, a production began to form from nothing. We were constantly told that the show would develop from us, but we didn't understand what that meant until a show was pieced together in two months with no theme or direction, just raw talent. The third month was finalized with dress rehearsals as we learned how to set up and tear down the stage. We became our own roadies and had the privilege of learning from professional lighting technicians, audio guys, and prop masters in the "biz."

Natalia and I used to joke that Madonna "ain't got shit on us" because she had others do all her hard work. During those first three months, we were practically inseparable. On one of my rare phone calls back to Germany, I told Doug all about her.

"She is so pretty, and you should hear her sing! She said if she were to sleep with anyone in the show it would be me or this other dude, but he is a total queen! I don't know how she can't see that! He is so fucking obvious, but she is head over heels for him. I don't get it."

"So, do you think you will get to bang her?" Doug asked.

"God, you are so vulgar... but I sure am going to try." I said, my voice turning sinister.

Always the pervert he replied, "That's my girl. Do you think she will want to do me or a threesome?"

"I don't know. Gross, I'm not trying to pick up girls to bring home for you. Get your own hoe."

"You can't hook a brotha up?"

"Gross. Get your own. I got to go practice, but I love you, honey. I'll call back in a few days."

"Okay, how much do you love me?" He waited for the familiar answer we shared in our three in a half year marriage.

"Theez much." I exaggerated.

"Do you miss me?"

I didn't think before I answered him. With much regret, I said, "No. I mean, honey, I am busy from the time I wake up to the time I get home. Then I practice on my own before I go to bed. I don't have time to miss you! I'm just on the go all day long."

Doug was silent at my unexpected honesty. I tried to lessen the hurt I had caused, but it only made the dig worse. "I mean, I miss you of course but I'm glad I don't have time to think about it, or I would be miserable, you know?"

"Yeah, well I miss you... a lot." His saddened tone was heartbreaking. I had made a huge mistake.

"I'm sorry," I added, but it was too late, the damage was done.

"I know you have a lot going on, but I miss you, and I love you." my loyal husband confessed. We talked about the scheduled shows and made plans for Doug to watch a performance at the Arizona venue, our old stomping ground. We ended the call on a much lighter note with words of love and a few shared giggles.

A few weeks later our opening night filled every seat in the theater. Nearly every show thereafter packed the house. The entire Soldier Show cast, including technicians, traveled on buses to each venue across the states. These long trips afforded Natalia and me plenty of time to bond.

My subtle hints to show interest in more than friendship were not exactly received. I did things like open doors, buy little gifts, inconvenienced myself for her sake, and doted over her every move. Armed with the knowledge of her onetime lesbian experience, I took things extremely slow. My intent was not to scare her away. When I openly expressed my feelings once, she brushed it off as if it was a joke, but she let me flirt a little and continued hanging out with me. When we finally had time off at selected venues, we dined in sushi restaurants to relax. This became our tradition and my wonderful excuse to spend quality alone time with her. We started calling our little excursions "dates" and sometimes extended them with shopping or a movie. On a few occasions, we held hands. Each outing ended with a hug and a kiss on the cheek. For Natalia, we were really good friends. For me, we were hiding a budding connection. This behavior had been consistent since the beginning. It was only a matter of time before someone made the first move. Unfortunately for me, Natalia was completely shitfaced during our first kiss.

It all started with a plan to visit the local mall in the next city near our venue at Fort Carson, Colorado. Gordon, one of the cast members, acquired a rental car and asked Natalia to accompany him. His obvious plan was to get Natalia alone, but she requested my company. Gordon was not happy about the idea of a trio; however, if he wanted time with her, it had to include yours truly.

He picked us up near our rooms and the three of us drove to the local mall in a town outside of the military installation. We shopped until our stomachs cried for the food that we smelled permeating from an upper scale restaurant attached to the mall. The three of us ate on the back patio nestled perfectly in the mountains. We had a wonderful time laughing and drinking the evening away until we realized the servers were folding chairs in preparation to close.

Giddy from dinner drinks, we decided we should visit a local bar to finish out our fantastic evening. A club was more my scene, but I was willing to try something new. They were ecstatic about my willingness but disappointed with my clothing.

Natalia pinched at my shorts and pulled the fabric out to wave it back and forth. "Girl, you cannot go into the bar with those shorts on. You look like a skinny person who used to be fat. The top is cute, but the shorts should be shredded," She giggled and flapped the material some more so Gordon could see what she was talking about.

Gordon asked, "Did you buy anything at the mall to put on? The shorts are too big," He was trying to be polite about it.

"Fuck you guys! I like these shorts. It's all I have, so whatever," I defended myself.

Natalia shuffled through her bag from the mall. "Here, I'll put this skirt on, and you can wear the one I have on because it matches your shirt." She ripped the tag off of the new skirt with her teeth and handed it to me so she could toss the bag out in the nearest garbage can.

"Oh, hell no! I don't wear skirts. Especially a fucking mini, are you kidding me? It's just a bar." I pushed the idea and the skirt back to Natalia.

Gordon chimed in with enthusiasm, "Yeah! Put on the skirt; you will look hot!"

"Gordon, I cannot dance in a fucking skirt. Let's just go. Who cares?" I pleaded with both of them. They laughed as they pushed me from the patio to the restaurant bathroom and forced me to wear Natalia's skirt, which was so tight it changed my natural gait and pissed me the fuck off.

"Guys, I can't walk. I hate you," I said, right before Natalia and I posed for photos with Gordon's camera. I tried to sit in the back seat of the rental but couldn't get comfortable no matter which ass cheek I leaned on, so I lifted the entire skirt around my waist and placed my shopping bag over my legs in embarrassment. "You guys suck. I am so fucking uncomfortable," I pouted.

Gordon tried to adjust the rear view mirror with hope of catching a peek, but I flipped him off with a smile on my face. He laughed and reset the mirror for the road.

The drive was short, and the bar was already packed by the time we arrived. I continued to tug at the skirt even after we sat down at the only open table. Natalia leaned over to me and whispered, "See, people think you look hot in that skirt."

"No, Natalia, they think I'm a prostitute," I said sarcastically. Gordon handed us our drinks as she threw her head back in laughter and tossed her long brown hair behind her back.

We didn't stay long, but it was enough to throw back a few shots before we headed back to base.

Gordon drove, Natalia was in the passenger seat, and I was seated in the back, definitely the third wheel. It's a bad combination for any group in their mid-twenties. When booze, dudes, and women get together, the guys always want more. In my experience, even sober in a high school cafeteria, boys sought sexual pleasure in innocently sharing ice cream. Connie and I didn't see anything provocative in passing a cone to the other one to try, but the boys did. They wanted to see us lick the cone at the same time.

Why did we do it and let them take a photo? Because it boiled down to money and there is absolutely nothing sexual about cold hard cash. Gordon was no exception to the horny guy rule. He wanted to see us kiss after about seven minutes into the drive.

I wanted to kiss her but certainly not for his pleasure. With a little coaxing from Gordon, she unfastened her seatbelt and leaned over the armrest for a smooch. It was all done in fun, but then she became more serious and leaned in for a second, more sensual one. Apparently, it was so good she squealed with laughter as she fumbled her way to the back seat for more. Gordon fought off her chunky heels as he tried to stay on the road without getting kicked in the eye.

Natalia was doing it to impress Gordon, of course. She would kiss me then report to him that I was a good kisser and tasted like licorice, courtesy of whatever mixed drink I had from the bar. She reported that my boobs were small yet firm and that my nipples were very hard and how she wanted to lick them.

She pulled down my tank top to expose my right breast and flicked my nipple with her tongue like a man in a porno. She made sure Gordon could see us through the rear view mirror. Then Natalia turned to me and sucked on them as if she was finally doing it for my pleasure. But of course, Gordon had to fuck it up and say some shit, just like a man would. "Why don't you go down on her?"

Natalia immediately sat up and adjusted herself to a proper seated position. "I don't give honey; I just receive."

I tucked my boob back into my shirt. "What!"

Natalia explained what that meant while she feverishly searched the bottom of her purse. "Look I was only with a girl once, and I don't do that, ew, I only receive. So gross." She opened a pink compact and blotted her nose. "But I love making out." Natalia snapped the compact closed and tossed it into the bag. She leaned into me. "You are a really good kisser."

My intent was to make a liar out of her, but the car stopped so we stopped. We had no idea where we were. Gordon could have driven deep into a canyon and murdered us both; we were that oblivious. Instead, he explained that we were at the Garden of the Gods which provided a beautiful view at night.

Like drunken nymphs, Natalia and I followed him through the pathways until we found a suitable spot for viewing which turned into a suitable spot for sex. At one point, Gordon tried to lean in for a kiss but was surprised when my arms pushed hard enough to make him stumble backward. "I don't want you. Don't touch me, okay."

"So, what can I do?" He asked.

I pointed to Natalia. "Her."

The beautiful bold moon lit everything perfectly as she gave me oral. The rocks dug through the material of my shirt which remained on my body. Natalia's shirt was pushed around her rib cage; her bra barely hung onto each shoulder. Gordon was fucking Natalia from behind, with his hands on her scrunched mini skirt. I tried to look at her without him in the picture. Natalia's long brown hair and tits pulsed with every one of Gordon's thrusts. They seemed to be millimeters away from popping out of her bra. They were so round and perfectly shaped they almost looked paid for. I wanted her bouncing boobs to be my last image before this whole debacle ended, so I closed my eyes and reopened them to the twinkling stars. Staring completely numb is a total understatement.

What the fuck was I doing? I tried to let her tongue make me feel good, but Gordon was pumping so hard that poor Natalia struggled to keep her mouth over my clit. She began fingering me, but that turned into fast jabs with every Gordon thrust. I made sex sounds in the appropriate places like the ladies in the pornos, but it hurt. It was like Doug-sex without lubrication, only worse. It burned; it stung.

The booze was beginning to lose its effect. There was pressure and ripping of thin, tender tissues, yet I let it continue until Gordon came and she slumped over me.

The three of us dressed and walked back to the car in silence where Natalia threw up the contents of her stomach on the sacred ground. Gordon drove us to a gas station so she could clean up. What a fucking gentleman.

On our way through the concession area, Gordon pulled me to the side to tell me that I must have started my period because there was blood dripping down my leg. It was bright red, almost to my knee, and partially dried. I scurried quickly to the bathroom where Natalia was walking out of the stall wiping her mouth on her forearm. As I washed my leg with a wet paper towel, Natalia asked me what happened.

"You cut me. You bitch." I scrubbed harder to get the dried part off.

Natalia rinsed her mouth out with water and apologized a million times with slurred words which included reminding me that she was drunk before she wobbled out of the bathroom with her hand over her eyes. It was a very quiet ride back to our rooms.

After showering in my hotel room, guilt and confusion wove itself into the emptiness I felt. It was not supposed to happen the way it did. I hated Gordon for being there and hated Natalia for doing it for his entertainment. But no one forced me to participate.

By the time Doug visited Arizona, I already confessed the sex with Natalia. I cannot remember if I omitted Gordon's participation because it was petrifying or because it was unimportant due to the lack of physical contact.

Either way, I was preoccupied with the way Natalia was ignoring me and how she was having some sort of mental breakdown. She took the opportunity to see a mental health professional the very weekend my husband flew in from Germany. This meant extra rehearsals to cover her solo numbers during the time I was supposed to share with him. One night, after a late rehearsal I secretly watched her sneak off with some guy while having a smoke break.

"That skank-honeia just left with some dude. She looks all dressed up to go out too. Of all the fucking times she could see a professional she picks the one weekend you are coming, and here she is going on a date. Breakdown my ass. Look, you can still see her walking to his car!"

From his relaxed position on the bed, he said. "Janell, get away from the window and just forget it. You should be happy because I am here."

"I know. I am. She's just ruining it though. Pisses me off."

"It's not that serious, Janell." Doug ended my bitch session with a reality check and a smile.

After weeks of rejection from my only confidant on tour, loneliness forced me to befriend one person who disgusted me. His name was Aaron, and he was an asshole. No one on the tour understood his sarcastic humor enough to get close. He was happy being a jerk. Just when you thought he was an okay guy, he would say some degrading shit, instantly making him asshole Aaron again.

However, it was sunburn that broke him to a small level of vulnerability. Apparently, he fell asleep face down near a pool and fried his back. In constant pain, he begged for someone to smooth aloe over the seared skin. No one offered sympathy but me. After volunteering, the routine ran twice a day for quite some time even after it peeled dead skin away exposing new pink flesh. It lasted nearly twenty minutes each time because it had to be executed very carefully. In all honesty, he should have seen a doctor, it was so bad. Aaron began to speak to me on another level during our aloe appointments and was actually a nice guy. Then as soon as his shirt was on again, he turned into instant fuck-tard. There was deep, sincere hatred for each other yet before long we sat together to share life stories. I reluctantly admit we had our moments of laughter, but I assure you, in my head, his untimely death was planned in so many ways.

It was a strange relationship. We argued in the wings, during rehearsals, and vocal practice. We never agreed on anything unless it was alone time, sleepy time, or joke time. We yelled at each other during the set-up of production lights and tear-downs. At some point arguing wasn't enough, so we became physical.

His verbal abuse was not going to go unnoticed. I demanded respect from him when he threw temper tantrums, which were often. Once, Aaron became angry when a bolt wouldn't loosen enough to disassemble the front lighting grid so, in a fit, he threw a ten-inch steel bolt wrench near my foot. I immediately screamed at him *what the hell is wrong with you, fucking psycho* before charging him with a hammer in my hand. At the last second my hand released the hammer enabling me to push him on his ass where he flipped over the grid that was propped on the floor.

"I'm sick of your shit and your god damn temper tantrums!" My scream was fierce and direct. The hammer near my foot moved as I lunged forward. Instinctively my grip constricted the handle. "You want me to throw this mother fucker at YOU?!"

Aaron tried to get up as quickly as he could, but the grid mangled his limbs. His face flushed angry red to pale white then to red again. "Fuckin' bitch, I'll kill you!"

The rest of the crew who initially stopped to investigate the commotion dropped what they were doing and ran over as fast as they could. A technician restrained Aaron before he could get his balance. Someone grabbed my arm but not in time to prevent my lunge and my free hand from slapping him across the face. Considering this was a military function with all ranks in the crew, we could have been in serious trouble. It was assault by both parties.

They told Aaron to take a break and moved me to do lights in another section. We ignored each other at every passing moment, however, on stage, the show must go on. Our audiences were none the wiser. We smiled and danced hand in hand as if we were a Disney on Ice couple.

The stress of the shows began with lack of sleep and the eventual seven bus breakdowns including a major five car accident somewhere in Delaware. We were away from our support networks of family and friends which made dealing with personal issues very difficult unless you had a friend on the tour. It's no surprise these semi-forced relationships always cracked.

When Aaron finally apologized on his own, it was obvious he needed my friendship to make him feel part of the team again. Notice he didn't necessarily want it. I accepted his apology, and, for a time, things were good between us, then it was back to arguing as usual. It never got physically abusive again, but it did get physical.

If the good Lord and baby Jesus could tell me why the hell we slept together, I still wouldn't believe him. There was absolutely no chemistry! There was no compatibility on top of the fact that we wished horrible deaths upon the other. So, when I cried about it, guilt-ridden for cheating on my husband, justification became the pressures of the show and Natalia's rejection. We continued to argue and express genuine hatred after it happened. Then we did it again, and I was horrified. My roommate suspected more infidelity despite my denials. My proclamation was that it was not going to happen again because of marriage. Additionally, Aaron was an abomination to mankind! My plan was to forget him. Out of mind, out of sight.

Separation worked until Aaron surprised me one night with a knock on my motel door at one of the venues where I had a room to myself. It transformed into an opportunity to rebuke his name.

"What the fuck do you want, Aaron?" I angrily said through my teeth as he stood in the hallway.

"Shut up, we need to talk," he stepped forward in an attempt to grant himself access to my room. I pushed the door closed, but his foot had made it a few inches across the threshold which was the only reason it actually stopped short from slamming in his face.

"No, we don't. I'm going to bed. Move your foot."

"Why are you being a bitch? Just talk… let me in." He blinked blankly and waited.

With seething disgust, I released the pressure on the door and turned to sit on the corner of the hotel bed. "What?" I pressed both hands into the mattress and straightened my elbows.

"What's your problem?" He gently shut the door behind him.

"I fucking hate you, Aaron. You are a prick." With arms crossed I stood to meet him at eye level so he could see how much he disgusted me. "I'm not sleeping with you again. I have lost my mother fucking mind… I'm married, I can't stand you, and I have no idea why I did that."

"Good." Aaron was very matter of fact. "That's exactly what I wanted to talk about."

"Well good for you. Get the hell out of my room," I directed.

"Jesus, I'm not a total dickhead. You must like me a little to sleep with me."

"It's called being lonely, Aaron. That's all that was. Are you done?" I cocked my head to the side and placed both hands on my hips.

"Why did you sleep with me?" His demeanor changed, and I believe asshole Aaron left his own body. What remained was a nicer sensitive version.

My tone softened to accommodate the new person standing before me. "I honestly don't know. Why do you put on such a front?"

"I don't know. Maybe it's a defense."

"You hurt people Aaron, with your words and your tantrums. Get it together man. One of these days you are going to step to the wrong person, and they will fuck you up, no questions asked."

"I know. You're the only one that tells me this shit. I didn't think it was this bad."

"It's that bad man. I can't stand your ass, but I know there is a good person in there somewhere." I pushed my index finger into his pectoral muscle.

Aaron smirks, "I can't stand you either. All right, sorry to bother you. I am leaving. Can I get a hug?" He held his arms open and looked at me with sad puppy eyes.

I reluctantly gave Aaron a hug, which turned to sex. Immediately afterward we argued. He called me a cunt after the belt I threw cut his face. I wished many morbid deaths to come his way, but we never, ever did that again.

Natalia's attempts to cheer me up became few. The stress of the show, long hours, bus rides, unfamiliar bug ridden hotels, transportation breakdowns, and the accident months before had everyone on edge. We were exhausted. When Natalia aka "skank-honeia" had the time to engage in happy conversation, I took it for more than it was worth. Maybe that's why she didn't talk to me as much. My belief was there was something going on between us that we had to hide. So, I dismissed her coldness as some sort of lovers spat that was 100% nonexistent to her mind. It wasn't until after September of 2001 when the twin towers of New York fell that she began talking to me regularly.

Our tour continued, but once we arrived at our new venue, we were on lockdown until further notice. Luckily for us, the venue was the Presidio of Monterey in California. What a fantastic place to be on lockdown for an unknown length of time minus the shitty circumstances.

Our accommodations were three blocks uphill from the docks, where seals could be heard barking at night. I'm sure with the weather as perfect as it was for that time of year the docks were a busy place most days, but it was exceptionally quiet after 9/11.

There were no people walking the docks, no boats and their horns, no cars looking for parking or pedestrians trying to find their way. All of the novelty shops on the boardwalk were locked up with shades drawn. The colorful pinwheels outside of some of the little kiosks which would have been desired by visiting children spun in the wind. Rainbow streamers blew and flapped in the direction of the water that gently licked the base of the dock. The charming, warm place was sad and empty. People vacated every inch of the little town either out of respect or fear.

Natalia and I ignored our lockdown order and snuck out one mid-afternoon to see the town in search for a place to eat. We walked for what seemed like two hours to find a place that was actually open. Luckily it was a sushi restaurant, which we had grown accustomed to finding at each venue with a scheduled extended stay.

On the exceptionally long walk through winding uphill roads we tried to talk about something other than the reality of what may happen as soldiers in the Army. We actually started smiling and laughing at ourselves, something that seemed taboo in the wake of 9/11 when the alarms from the fallen firefighters were beginning to fade forever.

The possibility of being pulled off of the tour to be soldiers in combat weighed heavily on each cast member from the moment we became aware of the situation. It had been four days; laughter seemed a forbidden fruit. But we did, and it felt so good we were actually giddy with it.

The restaurant was more upscale, but they let us in with our shorts and sneakers because it was empty. The waiter walked us to our table, a huge crescent-shaped booth meant for a large family. We scooted in from one side, shimming our butts over the fake leather to the innermost bend of the table, giggling all the way. Natalia sat to my left but moved close enough for our arms to touch. The unfamiliar surroundings, the ice water, and the absence of people made everything cold.

Natalia inched closer to me. When the food came, she gave me instructions on how to use my chopsticks. We snapped a few photos of the momentous occasion before the piece of California roll fell from my amateur grasp. We talked and shared and laughed. Above us, traditional high pitched pangs of mandolins and flutes played from a stereo system hidden in the ceiling. From the kitchen, a television turned to the lowest setting, hummed the latest devastation in New York.

Trying to regain normalcy and happiness in the moments we shared was futile. I read into unintentional flirtation and was too comfortable. During a fit of laughter, my hand eventually rested on her knee. There were no attempts to move it or lean in for a kiss. Simply removing my hand would have prevented what happened next. In one unexpected, swift motion Natalia slapped my hand off of her knee as she attempted to muffle a shout, *"Don't* touch me in public!"

She looked left and right to see if anyone had seen my indiscretion. I gently placed my hands in my lap and sunk into the booth. We didn't linger on the subject; we moved on as if my behavior was that of a misbehaving child who foolishly cursed and was reprimanded. Immediately, she punished me and forgave the incident. By the time we left, that small moment in time had passed. Forgotten like so many other small moments in a day.

Of course, my cache of rejections was growing. I harbored those words in the back of my brain with the others: "Don't call me again. I'm *not* gay!" "You had your chance." "I'm sorry, but I am really into Rick." Natalia hurt me as if I had never met a girl like her before. I was becoming sort of a connoisseur at this old hat.

Edwyn Collins, British indie musician, hit the nail on the head with his lyrics to "A Girl Like You." Collins' song is the perfect background for how my rejection memories make me feel. The fantastic late sixty-ish percussion with seventies electric guitar rock riffs blend for a powerful, gritty heartbeat under his voice which is reminiscent of early David Bowie and Bob Dylan if they were lovers and produced a child. His voice is "sloshy and dry" like he chain smokes in shitty basement bars after a few shots of whiskey.

You give me just a taste, so I want more.
Now my hands are bleeding, and my knees are raw.
'Cuz now you got me crawlin', crawlin' on the floor.
And I've never known a girl like you before.

It makes me want to hunt these women down and blast it on the street from my car for retribution. There's a lot of pleasure in thinking of opening my car doors and waiting for them to come out of their homes to inspect the cause of the riff-raff. Once they realized it was me in a leather jacket, black raccoon eyeliner, and punk hair, I would give them a double fuck-you-flip-off with motorcycle gloved hands, fingertips exposed of course because that looks super badass when you are driving around in your... Honda? It makes sense in my "fuck you fantasy" so work with me here. Anyway, they would open their screen doors to ask, "Janell is that you?"

As I would stand next to my Honda with fingerless motorcycle gloves, the music would blast his song to disturb her suburban neighborhood. Picture me finishing the last burning puff of my smoke and flicking it on their carefully manicured lawn just as the electric guitar jams the peak of Collins' song. The idea of littering gives me so much internal rest.

Except with Rachel. For her, I would produce a cigarette AND lighter to smoke while the music annoyed wholesome families in their suburban oasis. She would run to me, having never aged past eighteen, wrap her arms around me and seductively inhale the smoke from my mouth ending it with gentle licks to my lips. And as my head would swim and everything moved in slow motion, Edwyn would scream with real intensity:

You've made me acknowledge the devil in me.

I hope to God I'm talkin' metaphorically.

Hope that I'm talkin' allegorically.

Know that I'm talkin' about the way I feel.

And I've never known a girl like you before.

I would separate the front of Rachel's robe and slide my partially exposed fingers in her, right there in front of God, neighbors, and husband watching from the kitchen window with a coffee cup in his hand.

Never, never, never, never.

Never known a girl like you before.

I would make her lick my fingers before I'd sit in the driver seat, lighting another smoke before driving off.

See what happens when one's apparently forgotten moments of rejection haunt them for over a decade? Someone save me. I need Jesus.

Chapter 10

After leaving the Soldier Show early due to knee injuries, Natalia sent two postcards and a letter telling me of her snorkeling adventures in Guam and how much she missed me. It was over, but she certainly sparked some repressed burning desire because shortly after my return to Douglas in Germany, I began to complain about the need for a woman in my life.

While folding clothes on the bed, Doug asked why I was whining. "What the hell is wrong with you?" Were his exact words.

"I don't know," I said, drawing the word out like I was a cranky, hungry four year old as I slumped over the bed, face down into the linen and freshly dried clothing.

"Well stop it. Are you going to start your period?"

"No. I think I need a girlfriend," I corrected with my face still smashed into the comforter. My statement was muffled, but he knew what I was trying to say.

"So, you are whining about it? Just go get one." Doug made it sound terribly simple as he folded a sweater using his chin to grab the fabric.

I straightened from my slumped position, face now full of blood. I could feel my hot, flushed cheeks cool again as I stood erect and slurped drool back into my mouth. "I feel like I'm missing something in my life." I balled a pair of socks and threw boxers on his pile. He was particular about his folded clothing, so the "his" and "hers" fold pile had become the norm. "I need a woman in my life."

"So, go get one," he reiterated then methodically picked up the balled socks and set them next to another pair that would later become a row.

"What are you going to do? Sit at home with your thumb up your ass while I'm on a date with my girlfriend?" I folded a pair of jeans and placed them in my drawer.

He giggled as he tossed a pair of his old boxers which I had taken over as my underwear on the top of my pile. "Sure, why not."

"Right. I'm married. That's ridiculous; I can't do that." I walked back to the bed and pretended to kick dirt on the tiled floor with my head slumped.

He giggled again as he adjusted his row of socks. "Whatever you want. As long as you are happy, I don't care what you do."

Continuing the childish routine, I bounced up and down to emphasize my point. "I need a woman." I stomped around in an irritable, frustrated attempt for attention before throwing myself face down on the bed again. My muffled whines made Doug snicker.

"I need pussy." I slobbered into the comforter.

Doug laughed as he poked me in the ass with a quick jab of his index finger. "I do too," he remarked.

Life went back to normal after returning from the Soldier Show. My six-year tour in the Army was over, and it was time to become a civilian— correction, a proud veteran. We moved to my sister's town in Ohio just outside of Cleveland and rented a really nice renovated duplex up the road from her place. While working as a graphic designer at a local print shop that paid eighteen dollars an hour, Doug applied to colleges in the area to get his Masters in Psychology. We were on our way to beginning our happily ever after. We were miserable.

Let's talk about this for a second; Ohio sucks. Fuck the Buckeye state. The perfectly manicured lawns and one tree per front yard with a ceramic goose near the bushes makes me sick. The cross-stitched "home sweet home" placards in the front window and soccer mom sport utility vehicles in the driveway are enough to make me stab myself in the eye with a hot French fry. Although the town we lived in was trendier and more youthful, it still reeked of "frat boy gone dad" if you know what I mean.

The Cleveland stadium was about a ten-minute drive without traffic from my front door. Our peaceful residential street would have cleared during a game had we stayed long enough to witness it. We moved to Vegas before we ever settled. Thank God Doug's brother, Rico, talked some motivation into us. Otherwise I would be wearing an eye patch with a fake diamond in the center and constantly explaining the French fry accident to fat housewives.

Rico, who got most of the Spanish genes but really looked Turkish, was a man who transcended beyond macho. He was hyper-masculine, vulgar, bold, and honest to the core. He was a stocky, well-built guy with one of those indented "butt chins." He traveled more than any business person I have ever known, so his clothing influences were mostly European and very flashy. He has been called a faggot because he waxed every two weeks and a pimp because he changed his phone number more often than anyone could keep up with. Doug called him whatever he wanted to in Spanish. I just called him Rico, or "Fucker," depending on my mood. Despite his shady life, his tactless monologues, which were many through the years, were always right. He was the king of offensive common sense. It is Rico who can be credited with our conversion from Midwestern misery to Vegas history.

During his one and only visit to the great Buckeye state, Rico gave us one such crude speech. He leaned against the doorway of the dining room as we sat at our table sipping cocktails. Ever the metrosexual, Rico crossed his left foot over his right forcing a hand in the pocket of his super tight fashionable jeans – which by the way were adorned with strategically placed bedazzled beads.

"They're not fucking women's jeans, Leva, get a fucking clue," he scolded us earlier when Douglas teased about the sparkles on his pants. "These are from fucking Italy, pinche. I paid three hundred dollars for these."

Doug's high pitched laugh complete with banging on the table drowned out my comment about his sassy pants. Rico was confidently smug. "Bitches like to see my cock." Then he said some vulgar shit in Spanish before telling us that we needed to get out of this corn-fed state.

Smartly he discussed schooling options at the University of Nevada, Las Vegas for Doug to include pros and cons of several schools Doug had already been accepted to. His sales pitch turned to entice me with all of the possibilities for graphics positions in a city where graphics and marketing dominate in neon signs. When he pieced everything together it all made sense, including the plethora of pussy that apparently came his way in droves.

We were sold; Doug told him we would leave in a month after my thumbs up. Rico, always living for the moment, jumped in, "Man, fuck a month. Don't be pussies. I leave in two days. I'll pay for your ticket. You can stay with me, enroll in your fucking classes before the semester enrollment ends, and set up a place for Janell."

Rico looked at me. "You can stay with your sister, right? Get all of this shit sent to Vegas when this Leva gets a place. There is nothing to wait for here. For what, the children of the corn to ass rape you on the way to grandma's house?"

With more vulgarity and disgust, Rico repeated his concern of getting ass raped on a farm in Spanish. "Nadie me va a poner su verga en mi culo en medio de una granja! Pinche Deliverance, y me cago en tu madre que si no!"

He continued, "I warn you though, once you live in Vegas, no other city compares. I don't give a fuck; you won't be able to live anywhere else if you leave it, I promise." He grabbed his genital area to adjust himself then sat at the table with us to explain further.

What a deal closer! Rico could sell ice to an Eskimo; well to a pretty liberal one, if his language didn't get him killed first. I tilted my head to the side and teased, "What exactly do you do for a living again?"

His response, "Ching so madre, I deliver fucking pizzas."

Douglas left for Vegas two days later, and I paid for a storage company to get our stuff the next week. I stayed with my sister and waited for his green light to drive to the city of sin. Being jobless has its perks for a while until you have watched all the reruns of Oprah and organized the canned goods in alphabetical order. Eventually, my ritual included borrowing my sister's work computer to surf the net and chat after she went to bed.

My favorite site was a gay connections chat room which I frequented. One night, while I was up late typing, my sister walked into the living room to find me on the couch with her laptop, giggling at the screen. I jumped.

"What are you doing?" she asked as she rubbed her eyes, pushed long red hair behind her shoulder and yawned.

I jumped and felt my heart burst into my neck. "Chatting online." I shifted the computer away from her. It was fear, and it almost felt like my heartbeat was thumping my neck from the inside.

"To who?" She reached over and turned the laptop so she could read the screen without my consent.

I was shocked and embarrassed. "A girl in Youngstown." I moved the laptop away from her again.

That's when she realized it was a gay chat site and asked, "What are you doing there?" She knelt by the armrest of the couch to get a closer look and pointed to the word *gay* on the screen as she pushed it back so she could see it.

"I like girls," I said, slightly defensive with a hint of humiliation.

Her face changed to bright-eyed awareness. "Oh my God, you're a *muff diver*? Does Doug know?" She was dead serious as her jaw dropped in amazement.

I laughed hard at her face and her use of that term. "Well I wouldn't say that, but yes, he knows. I can't believe you just said muff diver." I tried to muffle my laughter as it was nearly three in the morning.

"Well, who's the girl in Youngstown?" Sheepishly she asked with intense interest.

"I don't know. I just started talking to her tonight. I think we are going to meet up tomorrow for coffee and maybe go out."

"Oh my God, like a date?" She stood up from her crouched position to stretch.

"Yes, on a date."

Her arm swung across the front of her chest as she pulled it tight with the opposite hand. She held it for second then switched arms. As she pulled it, she noticed the computer I was using. "Oh my God, Janell, you are on my work computer. Here, use this one." She pulled out another laptop hidden under some magazines. It was an older model, but it was also a laptop where gay dating sites could be accessed without the risk of being fired. "Okay, don't stay up too late. I'm going to bed." She crossed her arms, yawned and returned down the dark hall to her bedroom where she snuggled herself and went to sleep. That was it, total unconditional acceptance. My sister, whom I lovingly referred to as "Beaner" until I realized it was offensive to Mexican Americans when I was twelve, didn't even flinch. She was officially cool in my book. Well, kind of; she will always be my dorky red-headed, spectacle wearing sister to me.

Supposedly eighty percent of couples split or divorce after living in Las Vegas. The origins of this research are unknown so don't ask me but it's probably true. Vegas is known as the city of sin for a reason. One cannot deny the history of the city ridden with crime, gambling, drugs, strippers and whores, exceptional wealth and incumbent poverty. All of which I seem to have experienced during my residency, but we are not to that part yet.

After moving, Douglas managed to land a job with a real estate company and was doing very well. I was working as a third party collections agent. It wasn't adding anything to the savings account, but we paid our bills. Respectively, Doug worked late hours learning state laws and putting together contracts. I was well... a fucking collections agent with a headset in a five by five cubical. If you have ever been called by a collector you know the familiar "This call is being monitored..." disclaimer, which we were required to say to each "client," about eighty times a day.

Once again, we were miserable, but our relationship was rock solid. We went out, we shopped, and we stayed in to watch movies and had dinner with his family. We were generally very happy. We even started paperwork to buy a house.

Then Douglas received his layoff notice with the unfortunate "new guy goes first" rule. The sad part was that the manager had just offered him a promotion over dudes who had been with the company for two years. I'm telling you, he is a smart little fucker. But always a forward thinker, he enrolled himself into the University of Nevada, Las Vegas, the next day. He was much happier in a learning environment anyway. Doug is not one to enjoy "grunt" work, even if it involves paperwork.

Meanwhile, I was stuck wearing business casual clothing borrowed from my mother-in-law and listening to debtors threaten my life if I called their homes again. Excuse me; their cell phones, that they somehow maintained while claiming they were so broke, they spoke to me from the darkness.

Some of my coworkers had been in the collections business for years. I quit after the longest six months of my life and applied for a nanny job with a company just up the street from our apartment. I lied on my application so as to be placed with a family quicker. With a flick of my pen, my resume included a year and a half of experience working with a child afflicted with an attention disorder. The company hired me a week later without a background check.

Every Monday, just as they instructed, I visited the office to see if they placed me with a family. Every Monday I was turned away. Unemployment is not fun especially for the second time, so two months later and still unemployed; I bought my first pair of stripper shoes.

The bills were behind, the refrigerator was empty, and regular jobs wouldn't have paid enough to keep us afloat anyway. Douglas was in school pulling a full schedule and mastering every subject. I volunteered to shake my ass with his blessing, which he granted the best way he knew how. "Bring daddy some money. A bitch is broke."

That was my green light.

Not every gentleman's club is the same despite their reputation for being seedy. But stereotypes tend to come out of truth, so my mission was to find one that had some sort of class. Yeah, kind of like a garbage collector who refuses to pick up a torn bag, it just didn't make sense. In Vegas, some clubs are small, and apparently, they do not believe in lights. I walked out of one establishment simply because the smell was unidentifiable. Others are huge and very intimidating with disorientating disco lights and multiple stages. Something in the middle of the two extremes would be perfect.

After stumbling upon an acceptable strip club, I put on a little lipstick in the car and asked to speak to the manager. The manager said he did not need shot girls, he needed day shift dancers, and he offered me a job on the spot.

I immediately corrected him with my application in hand, pointing to the requested position. He abruptly restated as if this wasn't his first time, "I don't need shot girls with zero experience serving alcohol. I need day shift dancers. Do you want the job or not?"

I thought about buying German potato salad for my empty refrigerator and said yes.

Oddly enough, I bought my first pair of stripper shoes at one of the big-name department stores at the mall. They were not the clear plastic ones with lights and a nine-inch heel, rather sparkling brown strappy shoes with a four-inch wedge. Until then, my shoe collection consisted of military boots, sneakers, and flip flops. This transitional shoe was functional and sexy. Not to mention should I snap the smaller heel, I couldn't afford new ones.

The classy and seductive little brown dress was in the same store. Well, it wasn't supposed to be worn as a stripper dress. It was actually a long trendy club shirt with an asymmetrical hem that sat just at the bottom of my ass cheeks. It too was sparkling from top to bottom.

On my first day, I was so nervous I went into work two hours before my shift technically started. This was an acceptable thing to do in this line of work. Believe it or not, some strippers have respectable day jobs or kids they want to protect, so they come in early to transform themselves into their alternate personalities. Mine was Shyah.

When the D.J. asked me what my name was, I hadn't even thought about it. Picking a stripper name is actually harder than you would think. It's part of the fantasy of your character. Shyah was a girl I befriended for a short time in Germany. She spoke English better than me and kissed me on both cheeks once as most people in European countries do. In a split second, the memory of her became my personality simply because her name was not taken.

The D.J. announced, "Gentlemen, please welcome to the stage, for the first time, Shyah!"

The men clapped and smiled, the other girls clapped and smiled. I smiled and walked my exposed ass up the stairs to the stage. I was completely sober and just did it. Fuck it.

All of my stripper stories are priceless really. How can one choose a favorite from the multitude of anecdotes, which include getting paid in pennies to stepping on testicles to a three hundred pound man ejaculating on the back of my leg? After a while, each event became just another day in the life. It was the norm for Doug and me.

By that time, our pact to have an open marriage was normal too. He started dating his college tarts, and I started going to the gay bars after my shift. Hell, all I had to do was put on jeans and comfortable shoes.

Stripping did not make me promiscuous nor did dancing at the club. The sexual onslaught of women began after I dated Tracy, who was technically my first recognized "girlfriend." Our sad fling was like a test run for how things should not go in lesbian dating. After living through a miserable existence with her, things got wild, but she was the key to Pandora's box.

I met Tracy at the club. She was a feisty little Italian-gnome of a woman who was so much fun to be around that we started seeing each other. She stood to the grand height of four foot eleven, truly an Oompa Loompa compared to my five foot seven stature without the added four-inch stripper heels. She was butch with dyed blonde hair, loads of tattoos, and piercings all over her face. She looked like the perfect rebellious wild child who could take me away from the mundane life previously lived, which was perfectly acceptable when denying my sexuality.

I kept it honest, so she was always aware of my marriage. A friend dropped her off at my apartment once so I could finish getting ready for a night out. It was only once because she joked around with Doug and bit his ear so hard that she drew blood. I am clueless to the details, but all I heard was his yelping in the bedroom. She was one crazy Oompa Loompa.

I was always searching for someone else while seeing Tracy. It was obvious she was not a quality woman, so my online chatting had become an obsession to find one. Doug tried to understand my attraction to butch women; however, he never quite understood it. In fact, he became enraged one evening after looking at photos of a girl I was interested in. His anger came from how butch the girl was, almost manly. "Why do you want to talk to someone who looks like a dude? You have a man already," he argued as he bent in as close as he could to the computer screen to see more detail. He wanted to be sure it was really a female.

Butch women, androgynous women, appealed to me. Key note here, they are *women*. Although I do admit that some of them could fool a few innocent bystanders, they were ultimately my type. Ironically, at the time, the online term for a young butch lesbian was "boi," and God bless my heart, I loved the bois.

Tracy was most definitely a rebel boi. She liked me to call her Tray and paraded me around like arm candy at the club. She didn't have a job, but she always made sure a drink was in my hand by stealing money or swindling someone to buy it for us.

Tray moved from California after a car accident from which she received a monthly settlement check. She lived with a 56-year-old lesbian, for free, in an unfinished porch attached to a trailer. She was without a car, so we used mine. She was immature and almost always drunk, but she bought fake paper roses to give me with my own gas money. I guess that makes up for the time she stopped during sex to chug a beer then belched and tried to continue.

Sike. I didn't care about Tray, and she certainly didn't care for me. A better example of our jaded relationship was a separate incident when she answered her phone in the middle of sex and told me to hold on. Tray proceeded to tell the person on the other end that she would be right over. She hung up, got dressed, and went to fuck the girl that called.

Sex was so bad that I faked it each and every time for two months just to make her stop. She is the only woman I have faked it with in my entire life. It was a relief when she left, believe me. It was also a relief to heartlessly tell her it was over one night at the club. Strangely, the gnome cried, begged, and pleaded for my love in the parking lot. Apparently, she was so love-struck that a gay boy had to help peel her hands from my neck when I told her our relationship was a joke.

When I arrived home that night, Douglas was sitting on the couch watching a movie and sipping a beer. His date left moments before; the smell of her feminine perfume was still in the apartment. He paused the movie as I shut the door and immediately unzipped my boots to release the pressure to my aching feet. "How was your night?" He asked as I dangled one boot from the bunched seam at the toe of my sock then flicked it to the floor about three feet from me.

"Eh, I dumped her ass." I pushed off the other one with my sweaty sock and flicked it in the direction of its mate. Knowing he would want me too, I scooted each boot neatly against the wall.

Douglas watched me as he said, "Thank God, she was a twat. I got a B in my fucking Psychology class; I'm pissed."

When I joined him on the couch, we nonchalantly talked about his classes while I counted my tips on the coffee table. When it was time for bed, I peeled myself out of sweaty club clothes while Douglas carefully placed my boots on the shoe rack in our closet. My shower never felt so good.

The ease to which we lived our hectic lives was normal to us. It is easier to blame my transition into promiscuity on our comfort level with extramarital affairs than to admit I had just enjoyed being a hoe. Unleashing repressed sexuality was the next step and the only way to achieve this was to explore. Something about the city of sin gives good people permission to do bad things.

Desired is an understatement. It wasn't my features that made me attractive but my lack of involvement in love triangles. This fact makes an average girl beautiful in the lesbian world.

One wonderful aspect of Vegas is that it is a hub of cultural diversity. There were all types of beautiful women in all shapes and sizes. I was overwhelmed trying to pinpoint who I wanted to be with. The general rule was, if you were interested and I was interested, it was on. Especially, if they didn't mind the idea of me being married; this was always my disclaimer before it went any further than a first date. But girls who didn't mind are not exactly quality women. Hindsight is blind.

I made a lot of beer friends, you know, the type of girls that are fun only when they drink. They introduced me to more club heads that eventually networked me to Lindsey.

She was a hot Japanese butch girl with the most mysterious history. She was a very reserved wallflower. Her wardrobe consisted of worn Keds, baggie jeans, and an oversized black leather jacket that she never took off, no matter what time of the year. She dyed her hair a horrendous platinum blonde, and her only friend seemed to be a lanky old black guy with an afro. I told Douglas all about her as we laughed at her misspellings during an online conversation. Education is unimportant when it comes to sex; besides Doug was already my scholar.

Rayya, my closest beer friend, thought Lindsey was the ugliest thing she had ever seen.

"She's trash, Janell. Ugly chink trash!" Rayya, a heavyset butch girl, grew up in Iraq but claimed her Dominican side when she sensed a hostile crowd. Despite her mixed ethnicities, she really tried to live the life of an American, albeit a hick American with racist shortcomings.

"Lindsey is hot!" I immediately defended. Not every girl is for everyone; I get that. But she was attractive by many lesbian standards, not just mine. She would have been the catch of the day had she developed a better fashion sense. A sexy girl in a busted outfit equals ugly to a lot of women, but my philosophy was; the clothes come off.

She dismissed me with a head and eye roll. "Whatever. Fuck "sushi" if you want to. All I'm sayin' is stick with the white girls. White is right; don't get it twisted." Her head tilted to the side as if what she just said was gospel. Then she laughed as hard as I did.

"You are the most ghetto bitch I have ever met!" I managed through the kind of squealing laughter that makes your stomach muscles pinch up in pain.

Money was tight for everyone so a month later Rayya moved in with Lindsey and Afro man due to a financial jam. Or so she said. She called me in a panic a few weeks later and insisted I pick her up because she had "some seriously fucked up shit" to tell me about "sushi" girl.

She'd overheard Afro man talking on the phone about some "old bag" that had a heart attack during a home invasion. The woman had to be placed in intensive care, and Rayya explained how Afro man giggled about it to the person on the other end. She said he talked about his heart transplant and how he almost died when he had to jump from a second story window when the woman's dog attacked him.

Her first instinct after overhearing this was to snoop.

Rayya waited for him to get off of the phone and leave before she began some of her own investigative rummaging. She claimed to have found over twenty-five high-end DVD players stacked neatly in the garage under a tarp and some very interesting papers.

"Janell, what do you know about this girl? She's trash. Look at this." Rayya dumped a plastic grocery bag upside down on my dining room table and pulled out a state license from the pile. "Who's this bitch?"

Giggling, I grabbed the identification card out of her hand with an old photo of Lindsey smirking on the front. It was a painful smile really. She looked miserable. Her shoulder-length mouse brown hair was teased in an attempt to recreate an eighties style. The Pennsylvania ID captured Lindsey wearing huge thick glasses and a turtleneck that seemed to be very thick and suffocating. She looked to be about nineteen.

"She said she was from New Jersey," I frankly noted.

"She also said she was twenty-six! Do the math; she looks good for... thirty-three!" Rayya pointed out the birthday printed on the front. Then she pointed out the name on the card. "I didn't know you spelled Lindsey that way." In clear black print, the name on the card was April.

"What the fuck!" My mouth was open in shock as I sifted through every piece of paper.

"She's the home invader! She stole that lady's bird; sold that fucking thing on eBay." Rayya slapped another ID on the table with a different name printed on the front. "You know, one of those exotic rainbow birds that talk. She brought it to the house, Janell and tried to feed it crackers and tuna! It was loud and Lindsey – or whoever this bitch is – tried to give it some drugs to sleep! She stole the poor old bag's pet after giving her a heart attack. Who does that?"

"On eBay? They ship pets?"

"You mean stolen property! She was scared to death of that bird. Janell, she tried to give it water, and it bit the bitch's finger. I laughed so fucking hard. Serves her right stealing someone's pet bird. I thought it was odd that they got a bird like that if she was scared to death of it. Seriously who does that? I'll tell you who; crazy people and murderers." She crossed her arms and sat back in the dining room chair as if her statement was again gospel. She certainly believed everything that was coming out of her mouth. Her conviction when she spoke was genuine. "The papers said the invaders had animal masks on and I saw animal masks in Lindsey's room!" Rayya exclaimed with wide, worried eyes but without moving from the back of the chair.

In a black address book within the pile, there were at least thirty Vegas addresses. Some had what appeared to be account numbers written next to them. A few of the account numbers had passwords. The address of the old lady was crossed out.

"Shut the fuck up... she showed me Mardi Gras animal masks on webcam! I wondered why the hell she had them. It seemed so random." I looked closer at some of the papers with several other names on them.

"She's a crazy chink home invader. Good job. Read this; it gets worse." She handed me a three-page letter written from Lindsey to a girl who was her cellmate somewhere. Lindsey was apologizing to the recipient for an apparent sexual fling with someone else and asking for a second chance. The letter referenced a relationship of over a year and her beautiful green eyes.

"Ewe, she says she only dates women with green eyes."

She threw her hands high into the air. When they slammed down onto her thick thighs, they made a cracking sound. "Your eyes are blue. Great, a colorblind home invader. This just keeps getting better. You sure know how to pick 'em. First, Louanna the druggie and now a thief. Don't get it twisted!"

Before Rayya and I moved our friendship out of the club scene, Louanna was her butch sidekick. You never saw one without the other. They were both outstanding dancers and heavy socialites. But favoritism, dominated by appearances, was evident when they were known as the hot black girl with her fat Arabic friend. Louanna's athletic build, flawless skin, and killer smile tore them apart. Well, the girl they were both after tore them apart. It was the same girl Louanna left me for. This fact was the common ground that sparked a friendship between me and Rayya.

"Hey, I didn't know Louanna was a pill popper. I don't know the signs and symptoms of a druggie!" My defense sucked, but it was the truth; I had been totally conned by a thief and a drug addict.

"Obviously. Louanna told me she fell asleep during sex with you. I don't know how you didn't know she on something." Rayya puckered her lips and tilted her head to the side. This was her endearing smug face. The one she used when she spilled the beans on secret information. She completed the look with condescending sarcasm when she lifted one eyebrow.

I sat back in my chair, "When did she fall asleep?" and crossed my arms over my chest.

"When you had sex. She told me. I guess you were supposed to go to see the lights on Fremont Street or something. She said she took too many pills and fell asleep while you were going down on her."

"Holy shit, I wondered why she got so quiet! That bitch!"

When Rayya laughed, her mouth seemed to unhinge as wide as it could, and her whole body shook. Her head practically rested on her back as she laughed until she coughed. She was a very loud obnoxious laugher especially when it was at my expense.

"Lindsey is a coke head too, and afro man sells his heart transplant pills for money. Did you know that? I walked out one night, and the man was disgusting. Sweating and wheezing. Janell, he looked green. I didn't even know black people could turn green. I thought he was dying on his dirty home invader couch. He has a life-size photo of you in his bedroom too. Creepy."

The information caught me completely off guard, and when I jumped, I nearly fell over backward in my chair. "What!"

Her hands carved out an image of a door into the air then she mimed opening it with a knob. This imagery was some form of mockery as she explained it again only more slowly. "He blew up a picture of you, poster size, and has it on the inside of his closet door."

"I'm going to toss. We have to tell the cops."

"I ain't doing shit. I still live there. What are you trying to do, put me in the streets? That's if I make it to the streets, you know they got guns. Tell Louanna I got swindled by a chink and an afro and tell her I said goodbye at my funeral. Bye, bitch." She put her hand in the air and waved like a beauty pageant winner.

"Fuck Louanna." I crossed my arms again. This time it was in disgust.

Her laugh was extra loud. It actually scared me, and I jumped a bit when she slapped the table. "No, you fucked her. She slept. Don't get it twisted!"

Louanna and Lindsey were not the last of my conquests that were into having a permanent white line under their noses. They were certainly not the last to feed off of my lack of knowledge in the world of pills, crack pipes, and cocaine which was endearingly referred to as yay-yo.

There was the Hawaiian who thought it was funny to bang my stripper co-worker and make me smell her fingers while on shift.

And there was Monica the Mexican. I actually liked Monica much like when I first met Louanna. There was a connection with both women. It's a shame really. You could tell they used to be good people before their addictions.

Monica and I met at karaoke night in the gay bar. Karaoke drew a decent crowd on Wednesday nights, but there was ample room to move and hear a conversation. She came to my table to offer a drink while complimenting my singing. She was polite and funny. Any girl will tell you that the funny factor scores huge points and gets your foot in the door during the courtship process. She was a hippie chick with thick wavy hair and wore some kind of hemp necklace woven through seashells. She was from Mexico but spent the last seven years living in Hawaii right on the beach. Her accent had lost most of its Hispanic influences for Hawaiian slang, but her Mexican culture still thrived.

She was so fantastic I lost track of time talking until the karaoke host began packing her equipment around two in the morning. She completely understood the status of my relationship with my husband but still asked for my number. "Naw, it's cool, kid," she said with a wonderful straight white smile. The next time I saw Monica, it was the same fantastic connection in the same bar. We got to know each other for hours until it was time to leave. She escorted me out, and when we reached my car, we shared our first kiss. "I don't want to let this night to end, man. Let me take you to my place." She had her thumbs tucked under the belt on my jeans but nothing too forward or vulgar.

I accepted.

Her roommate and her baby were not there, so Monica asked me to stay the night after a fairly steamy make-out session. I said yes after I texted Doug my plans and took a shower. During sex, she wouldn't let me take off her clothes. She flinched upward when I attempted to unzip her pants and grabbed my hands. "No. I don't shave like you do," she said.

"I can't touch you at all?" I asked as I pushed her wild hair away from her face.

"It's all about you tonight, kid." She rolled me onto my back, and we continued to have sex on the floor, surrounded by baby toys. When I finished, I gave her a few kisses and turned to my side to fall asleep. She mumbled something that I couldn't hear, so I twisted my naked body around to her. My eyes widened in the dark when she repeated it again.

I half-jumped up and flipped over at the same time. "Did you just say your fucking girlfriend is coming home?"

"Bra... Yeah, kid, you can't stay. I just realized what time it is, man."

I was reaching for any clothing item I could recognize in the dark. I was frantic as I untwisted my underwear and grabbed my jeans. "What the fuck? How much time do I have?"

"She gets off of work in..." She looked across the room to a clock on the wall that I didn't notice. "Half an hour, man. I'm sorry."

"You're *sorry?* What the fuck Monica? You have a girlfriend! This is not okay." I snapped my bra closed and tugged my shirt over my head.

"Aw, come on kid, you have a husband."

"The difference is, *he* knows where the fuck I am right now." I walked out and drove as fast as I could back to my normal husband, my normal apartment, and the stable life I knew. Crazy as that sounds.

It was a month or more before I bumped into an overly apologetic Monica. She told me that the relationship was in its final stages when that happened, and she had since moved out. Her Latina charm worked some kind of voodoo magic on me so I agreed to an official date so she could make it up to me. She picked me up on her new motorcycle and introduced herself to Doug. They chatted in Spanish, cracked jokes, and she shook his hand before we left for a nice restaurant in one of the casinos. You know, one of the places where the drinks are pieces of colorful alcoholic art in opulent glasses.

After dinner, we rode back to the hotel where she was temporarily living to drink some more. Then she decided she wanted to take me to a strip club of my choice because I apparently didn't get enough of the environment at work.

On the way to the strip club, a cop pulled her over for speeding. I sharply told her to keep her mouth shut while the officer was running her insurance. She was a Hawaiian influenced, drunk hippie with a Mexican attitude on a speeding motorcycle. The way she was talking to the cop sounded like she had been smoking pot for hours and had ferocious munchies. When the cop let her go with a warning, my blood pressure returned to normal.

Onward we drove to the strip club where she consumed another three or four beers and two shots while I got a lap dance. After the dancer walked away, I leaned into Monica to let her know it was time to leave. She was fidgeting uncontrollably and asked one of the shot girls if they knew where she could buy some cocaine; aka yay-yo.

"What the fuck are you doing?" My face scrunched with anger.

She couldn't keep her head still, and it swirled as she spoke. "Bra, I'm fucking drunk. I need some coke to wake me up so I can drive, kid."

"You are not doing drugs on our date!" I didn't know what else to say.

She tucked her wild hair behind her ear and leaned in to try to whisper to me, but it was just as loud as if she had shouted it. "I just need one bump so I can ride. I'll do it in the bathroom; then we can go; it will wake me up." She meant to sit back in the chair, but the booze in her system forced her to throw herself at the back of the seat. She bounced awkwardly before her whole body leaned to the left.

"I would rather walk home from here. If you do it, I'll walk. Just sit here for a while and sober the fuck up. I can't believe you want to snort coke so you can drive! That's your fucking answer?" I held my hand out to receive her keys completely prepared to walk if I had to, but she handed them to me along with her wallet in good faith then she reluctantly drank water for the rest of the night. It was maybe an hour and a half later when I hesitantly mounted the back of her motorcycle to head for the gay bar.

It was karaoke night there, and I insisted she get something to eat before we drove the rest of the way. My apartment was over fourteen miles from the strip club, but so help me God, I would have walked home. At least if the night got any worse, the walk from the gay bar was less than six.

When we arrived, Monica ordered a pizza and chilled out in a booth while I sang. A gay couple was so impressed they offered to pay me twenty bucks to sing another song as we were preparing to leave. I looked to Monica, she looked to me, and we waited to go up again. After the second song, I chatted with the gay couple for about fifteen minutes until my scans of the club for Monica were beyond futile.

After returning from the bar, I asked the boys. "Have you seen the girl I was with?"

"Sure, she was talking to someone in the back while you were singing. She is probably in the bathroom."

I waited nearly half an hour before scouring the place to look for her. My gut told me what must have happened, but my heart desperately ached for my hunch to be wrong.

Back at the table with the boys, I didn't quite know how to express the gravity of the situation. Staring at the swirling disco ball on the dance floor, I said, "I think she left."

I starred at it a little too long before one of the boys spoke up after whispering to his boyfriend. "Oh honey, she is probably in the bathroom."

"Nope, I looked." My voice was monotone as I let disco sparkles dance in my eyes.

"Well she couldn't have gone far," he reassured, but his partner reminded him that the pizza was gone.

My eyes left the glittery ball and broken reflected lights to see the grease spot on the table where the box had been. The shining oils picked up the reflected lights from the disco ball. Without moving my eyes from the grease, I mumbled, "How will I get home? I didn't bring any money."

A tender hand warmed the top of my shoulder. "Honey, she is probably sleeping it off in the car."

"She has a motorcycle, and if it is gone, she left me here on our date." On autopilot I got up to check the first parking space to the left of the entrance—just as I suspected, it was empty.

Frozen in disbelief, and then reanimated by a slow-burning anger, I returned to the booth. One of the boys knew what had happened by the look on my face, but he asked anyway, "She left you?"

With direct eye contact, I said, "With no money, on a date and she took the fucking pizza." Through my anger I smiled just before my eyes began to water then I lost it; buried my face in my hands and cried.

The boys were kind enough to hand me a twenty dollar bill, all they had left, to help me out. They were staying in the casino up the street but had walked; otherwise, they would have given me a ride. They were worried that the money they gifted wasn't enough to get me home.

"I have no idea. I've never taken a taxi home before. I always drive everywhere. Thank you; I'll just walk from wherever he stops if it isn't enough." I wiped my face and sat with the couple smoking their cigarettes until my taxi arrived to take me as far as twenty bucks would pay for. I cursed Monica all the way home but cursed myself more for letting it happen.

The next morning, I explained the events of my evening to Douglas. He was seriously upset that I did not call him, but the bulky phone wouldn't have been practical in my tight pants on her motorcycle. I explained this to him as he stood over the dining table to pack his book bag in preparation for his afternoon classes. "Jesus, how do you meet these fucking women? I told you, date up, never down. The next one should always be better than the last." He pulled a notebook out from the bag and began picking off tiny lose paper edges from the metal binding. His face was scowling.

"Why are you getting mad at me? It isn't my fault; she's a twat and left me. And you date some dingy bitches too." I tried to deflect.

He stopped picking at the paper to stare intensely at me. "Because she left my *wife* in a bar alone! Don't talk to her again." He ordered before he began to tweeze at the torn edges for a second time. "Ditzy college girls are different from drug trash, and you know it." He made his point.

"You're right." He was always right. I yawned and crossed my arms over my chest as I shook my head and mumbled, "And… she took the fucking pizza." I waited for him to see the tragic comedy in it before we tackled together.

His high pitch laugh drowned mine out as he pointed at me to mock me with a grand gesture. "A bitch got left!" When his laughing fit finally subsided, we shared a few leftover giggles before he scooped the pile of discarded paper into his hand and kissed my forehead. "I love you." We hugged, and that was that.

So how do you find decent lesbians in Las Vegas, without a drug problem, who won't leave you at a bar, that will date a married woman? I turned to the chat rooms where there were quite a few gems.

Joy was one of them. She had recently moved to Las Vegas and didn't know too many people, hence the online networking. One night while chatting we cut the conversation short to get ready for the National Coming Out Day festival. We skipped the parade they had earlier in the day, but the evening events were sure to be a blast! This is how the conversation was typed:

NelliBean: so you would rather stay on the computer than meet me there?

CaddiesRCrazy: are you going?

NelliBean: yes. listen, get your ass off of the computer and meet me in person. *wink* ill be the one dancing on the pole.

CaddiesRCrazy: i have to shower and get ready

NelliBean: well I am leaving in like 20 minutes to get a parking spot. I hope to see you there!

CaddiesRCrazy: bye sexy

NelliBean: not goodbye… see you in a few.

I logged off, freshened up, and gave Doug a kiss goodbye. Then I drove to my favorite club where the street was closed off for the festivities.

The Gay Lesbian Bisexual Transgender (GLBT) community was out in full force, complete with sparkling outfits and rainbows galore. It felt like home. Even the smell of it was welcoming.

At the club, three dances into my night, I finally stood at the bar for my first drink. Just as the tequila finished burning my throat, my favorite songs began to play. As I walked back to the packed dance floor, a hand reached out from the crowd and grabbed my arm. There was Joy standing in all of her big girl glory with a smile from ear to ear.

She said, "You look much better in person." Her tiny labret piercing sparkled when she spoke. Squealing with delight, I immediately gave her a hug and dragged her to the dance floor. She absolutely lied when she said she could not dance. She may have been five foot four and 240 pounds, but she had moves and confidence. I was totally impressed with the whole package, not to mention her killer chops.

After walking outside to catch some fresh air, we stood near a booth with some other beer friends. It was a beautiful night, warm and bug-less as we joked and flirted. "Are you staring at my lips?" She asked after noticing that my focus was not on her eyes.

The vendors yelled into to the crowd to play their games as the club music poured out of the entrance of the club. "Yes, I always do that. I'm sorry; I can't help it." I smiled and tried to look into her eyes.

"You want to kiss me, don't you? You are staring again." Her laugh came from within as it passed over the labret piercing below her bottom lip. It was warm, honest, and hearty as she bounced with each chuckle and the piercing sparkled in the vendor lights. I never thought twice about accepting her request for a date a few days later.

Our first date was a different kind of debacle. Remember the phone call Tracy answered during sex? Well, somehow *that* girl had become an acquaintance of mine and Joy's through the chat room. We talked to Tess mostly online because we really didn't like her, and we certainly enjoyed talking about her behind her back. But we were not heartless, so we picked her up after a frantic call asking for a ride to the bus station about half an hour into our date. She wanted to go back to Tennessee and didn't know anyone else who could take her. When we arrived, she told us we had to wait until her roommate got back from work so she could unlock the back room. That's where her bags were. We never complained or said anything about the disruption of our date. We just rolled with it.

Tess and I eventually stepped outside to sit on the curb for a cigarette. As we bonded a little over the subject of sexuality, Joy sat in the apartment to wait for the roommate whom she apparently knew. This was becoming the lesbian triangle bullshit I managed to outrun thus far. Tess had a very thick southern accent. I don't think it originated from Tennessee where she claimed she was from, but it was most definitely a Deep Southern influence from somewhere.

The night was still and the perfect temperature for a long conversation on a curb. "I was married too, girl, and I had to let him go because I am gay. It's hard to come out, but honey, you are a lez-bee-yin. Own it, honey."

"I love my husband. I am never going to leave him. You don't understand the relationship we have, but I'm not leaving the women either. I'm good." I grabbed my legs to pull my knees up and match the back of my heel to the surface of the curb. It gave me a place to rest my chin.

"Oh honey, you are in the closet. You are gayyyy. You are so far in the closet you are like, back with the sweaters. Way fuckin' back." She looked away and fidgeted with her earring before snapping her head back to me. "You are soooo, gayyyy." She was frustrated, but I laughed.

Joy came out in the middle of my hysteria to tell Tess that her roommate was home. Tess walked back into the apartment to grab her things leaving Joy and me to sit on the curb.

"So much for our date." She giggled and tongued at the piercing on the inside of her lip.

"It's cool. I've had worse." I smiled. If only she knew.

"I want to kiss you right now, but I won't. We are out here alone, finally. The timing is too obviously perfect." She was absolutely right; we were finally alone. The night air was a comfortable temperature. There were no bugs flying around, no ants crawling on the pavement or critters anywhere.

"You are right. Wait for the perfect moment, not the perfect time." She was on the same page, so we high fived each other instead.

Then she played with her piercing as she said, "Since the night has been crashed, I figured we could kind of make it a girls' night out and bring Tess to the club since it's her last night in Vegas. I invited Nina to tag along. Is that ok?"

"Sure, we can go to my place for some pre-drinks. Doug is there. I want you to meet him."

On my first date with Joy, we spent an hour in my apartment with Tess, Nina, and my husband. Doug took photos of us and laughed at Joy's jokes. They were really getting along very well. When we finally left for the club Joy commented on how awesome she thought Doug was. This was going to be a good relationship.

At the club, Tess and I began setting up the pool table while Joy and Nina went to get drinks. We started talking about the chat room where we all met and how Tess came to Vegas for a girl. She explained that she was leaving because the relationship she thought was going to happen was a joke. "It was a mistake, honey, that's why I am leaving. So why are ya'll hanging out tonight?" She pointed to Joy who was, by then, walking two drinks to a nearby table with Nina right behind her.

I took the first shot, breaking nothing but my finger as it went crooked and into the air. "Well, we are kind of on our first date tonight," I said as I set myself up to attempt it a second time.

"Who? Ya'll? Oh, and I'm ruining it!" Tess shouted. As she walked over to Nina, who handed her a drink. Joy's eyes bulged from her head as she realized what was said and froze in her tracks. Nina asked who was on a date as she looked to Tess and me and sipped the first refreshing sip of her beer. I answered humbly, "Me and Joy. It was supposed to be our first date tonight." Then I looked to Joy whose eyes had impossibly widened further, frozen stiff with a drink in each hand. She had been caught doing something wrong, but I swear as I stared at her, unaware of the trouble she was in, a smile crept in the corner of her mouth. Nina slammed her beer on the table causing the head to spill over, slapped Joy's arm and stomped out of the club. Joy excused herself and rushed out after her.

Tess and I were clueless as to what had just happened, so we continued our game of pool without them. When Joy finally returned, she told us that Nina drove home. When Tess and I asked about the dramatics, she nervously adjusted her backward baseball cap as she explained it. "Well, we are kind of dating."

"That's your girlfriend?" I set the pool stick on the felt, more interested in hearing the whole story than angry.

"No, we just slept together once or twice and, you know, it's not serious. We were just kind of seeing each other, but I told her I didn't want to anymore. It's all good."

Tess took sips from her drink between each juicy piece of information and smacked her lips. "No, you did not. That is scandalous, honey." Then she turned to me to say, "God bless your heart."

I smiled because it didn't matter to me. She had consistently caused flutters in my stomach which was something I was not willing to ignore. "Can we resume our date now, please? I need another drink." I half begged but totally deserved it, and she knew it.

Joy chuckled and walked with me to the bar where we stood in line and shared our first kiss. It was so fantastic I pretty much had an out of body experience. It was soft and smooth and perfect. The room around us darkened. I watched myself kiss her as I levitated to the ceiling.

On our second official date, Joy took me to watch the planes take off at the airport. At night the runway lights shimmered as much as the famous lights of the strip on the other side of the chain link fence. It was beautifully fascinating.

As each aircraft passed, the thunderous engines sent vibrations through her sports utility vehicle. She had music playing low enough to talk over. We shared a wonderful time chatting, laughing and eventually making out.

About fifteen minutes into heavy breathing and the deep desire to go further, her cheeks flushed with arousal as she pulled away from our kisses with my hand still under her shirt. "Do you want to take this back to my place?" she politely asked. I said yes to which she added, "Good because my fat roll is getting cold." Then she pulled her shirt back down over her stomach and roared with laughter. My efforts to click the seatbelt together were hindered by the hysteria that ensued. She was so confident about her size. I loved that about her, and I was more than happy to share her bed if that's where she wanted me.

During the few sexual experiences I shared with Monica and Lindsey, who were both my size, they never took off their clothes. In fact, both of them were completely dressed every time, down to the socks. If they hadn't been ashamed of themselves, they could have pulled off the hot and mysterious fully clothed look.

Maybe that is the root of my infatuation with the full figured woman. They typically go with the sexual flow and ask fucking questions later. Maybe they get embarrassed about a little cellulite *after* they have an orgasm. Rayya once said, "You *know* there is a big bitch under this XXL shirt. It's not like I'm trying to hide that shit. Don't freak when you see stretch marks… because I'm getting mine. That's right!" She was my hero.

Doug asked me why the girls I dated seemed to get bigger and bigger after meeting Joy. I politely reminded him that he liked his ditzy, big-titty hoes and I liked my big butch bois who by the way were not on drugs leaving me at karaoke bars. Touché, he said and left it alone.

When Joy and I got to the point where sex was a given, her clothes came off just as fast as mine. She was playing fantastic R&B music on her stereo and even stopped every now and then to sing a lyric to me. She was comfortable, which made me comfortable… which made me very, very happy.

"Oh my God, what are you doing? It feels so good." I moaned.

She came up for air while her fingers continued to move inside of me. "I can eat a peach for hours." She shot a devilishly sexy smile and slowly disappeared between my thighs again.

This big bitch owned my pussy. Whatever voodoo trickery bullshit she was doing was absolutely working. Sweat was all over the sheets that were balled under my back. I grabbed the edges of her mattress and pulled so hard it curled. I felt an explosion beginning to happen, and just when it became unbearable, I demanded she stop.

"Please stop. I am going to scream." I pleaded.

"That's what I want," she said and moved her fingers again.

I flinched. "No! I am serious. I mean I am going to scream at the top of my lungs; you don't understand." Normally this wouldn't have been an issue, but her mother was trying to sleep in the next room, which really makes any sexual experience a little uncomfortable.

To clarify things, I truly meant like a high pitched murder victim scream in a bad horror film. Every sensation across my body was unbearably overwhelming, and I just couldn't take it anymore. My pussy was on strike and brought its own blow horns and picket signs; I was done. With much hesitation and frustration, she stopped. She crawled up the bed to lie next to me as my body relaxed. We looked at each other for a few minutes until my breathing was normal again.

After complimenting her skills, she smiled and said she needed to go wash her hands. Naively I asked why. I wanted to fall to sleep just as we were. She gently lifted her hand and separated her fingers, showing me the glistening cum that attached itself to each digit like webbing.

"Oh my God, what is that? I don't have an infection!" I blurted in a panic.

Confused, her forehead and eyebrows scrunched together. "Um, that's cum. You came."

"I did no such thing! I don't do that!" I stared at her hand still in the air.

"Yes, you did." She turned her palm away to show me the back of her hand and bent her knuckles, breaking the matter that had dried.

"Go wash it off! I am so embarrassed." I grabbed the crumpled sheet and covered my head. She giggled as she got up and walked to the bathroom in her birthday suit. As I waited for her, I wondered if she was right. That never happened to me before in my life. The feeling came in waves for over an hour until I nearly shattered glass with my scream. Did I really experience my first orgasm at twenty-six years old? Even after receiving counsel from some older wiser lesbians, I was in disbelief.

Douglas and I talked about our dates the next evening when he came home from school. I was ecstatic to tell him about my apparent vaginal orgasm. He turned purple with laughter when I told him my reaction, but he thought it was cute and hugged me while mumbling something about becoming a woman.

As much as I liked Joy's confidence and embraced my preference for thicker girls, I was embarrassed when she wanted to take me to the club. We were such an odd-looking pair. However, I began the process of retraining this shallow way of thinking. But unbeknownst to her, I began breaking things off with several women so we could be exclusive. My goal was to get over the superficial idea that thin women were what I should fancy versus what I actually liked. It wasn't going to happen overnight, but I was willing to start somewhere. It was a stranger at the bar who helped me see the light at the end of the big girl tunnel.

God bless the stranger who shared the same space as me and engaged in small talk. As we sipped our drinks and admired a group of women, she inadvertently changed my life. We discussed which one we thought was attractive. Within that short conversation, I pointed to the Italian girl in the green shirt surrounded by feminine women, and a second butch girl. Green shirt girl was laughing and drinking her beer as one of the femme girls walked over to sit on her thick Italian lap. This was the moment when the stranger immediately said some profound shit, "Ah, you are a chubby chaser."

I'll be damned; the ownership of that label pushed me over my insincere limitation. It helped my defense when Doug and Rico criticized the various large women I fancied. Their favorite sneer was *you can do better than that* as if a bigger girl was less than beautiful.

"I'm a chubby chaser. That's what I like so suck it," I told the boys. Even Doug admitted that Joy was a very nice girl after his brother left.

It took me a month to dump all of the other women before I threw myself at Joy's feet as a willing exclusive partner, minus Doug. When the nerve built itself into a request for a relationship on the phone, she told me she was sorry but that she had to turn in her player's card. She'd met someone else and planned to start dating her. But, she explained, we would always be "holla back girls," aka fuck buddies. I was officially a backup plan.

Surprisingly it didn't cause friction. Joy was too awesome to forget. Being her friend was okay with me; I was married anyway. What lesbian wants to date a married woman even with a husband as cool as Doug? Let's be real here.

However, yours truly was determined to find a girl who would be accepting in a relationship of that nature. I was sure she was out there somewhere. That's when I began to read books on bisexuality and discovered the research of Alfred Kinsey.

Books helped clarify a few things for me and Douglas. We read chapters to each other that we thought pertained to our lives. One of them mentioned polyamorous relationships. That is where you have committed loving relationships with multiple people. It can get very complex, but as long as everyone is aware of their status and everyone respects boundaries, it can work. If it all sounds very Utah polygamist, do the research, it is not.

An example in the book was of a triadic unit that consisted of a husband and his wife and her girlfriend who were committed to each other for over fifteen years. The husband never had a sexual relationship with the girlfriend. They all lived together and raised their children as three parents. There was another quadratic unit with three males and one female. The woman only had a sexual relationship with one of the men. The three males had been exclusive to each other for eight years until the woman became a part of their lives. Four years later, they were still together, and none of them stepped outside of the unit. Believe me; the research got more confusing as the geometry spanned into words I cannot pronounce. But, the possibility of this kind of life was very real for me and Doug.

When I met and fell in love with Patty and her sexy freckles, it seemed to be the life we researched. She accepted and wanted the type of relationship we eventually came to live. The three of us, of course, had rules. It was either me and Douglas or me and Patty. I was Doug's primary relationship, and Tasha was his secondary. We developed nights of the week that we designated for our respective partners. When jealousy issues developed, we dealt with them head-on. That's not to say they disappeared. I was constantly wrapped in guilt for splitting my time between both of my separate lives which became increasingly hectic.

My schedule was highly involved, and I am not talking about sex, not even remotely close.

To supplement stripping money, I joined the Nevada National Guard. Additional money also came from mud wrestling at a casino once a week. Patty and I enrolled at the local community college with full schedules. Topping the daily calendar was my marriage and my girlfriend. I was a busy bitch. This was a time in my life where being pulled in three different directions on any given day was a break from the usual seven.

If one item on the agenda was removed, we were lost and forced to focus on just how strange our polyamorous lifestyle was. A fine example of this was when Tasha ended her relationship with Doug. It gave him plenty of nights alone and time to think about the distance growing between him and his wife.

It was a shaky few weeks full of guilt. It had us questioning a lot of things, but he began dating again, which allowed us to continue. Three of the women met me under the impression that I was his lesbian roommate. Patty, Doug and I worked out a new wild schedule, and we moved forward with our lives, but it's a little more difficult for a man to be honest about his unusual relationship status to straight women.

It was one of those things he had to expose in a delicate manner with much finesse. He definitely struggled a little more than I did developing his place among our triadic unit. One of the women he dated was exceptional. Doug really liked her, but it ended when I sent her an email that was inadvertently tagged with my last name. She put two and two together, and that was it, she broke it off. After that, he began portraying himself as a single man. That is what Candice thought he was when she met him. His struggle to find a secondary relationship didn't just end there. He also had to make the lie believable. One morning I found every one of our framed photos in a drawer. He giggled like a child as he explained prepping the apartment when Candice came over on the nights I spent with Patty.

"I have to do a recon of the place and hide all of that," he told me as he pointed to the photos in the drawer and continued to fold down the bed.

"We have a one bedroom, where does she think I sleep?" I turned down my side of the covers and fluffed my pillow before slipping between the clean linen.

Doug dimmed the light on his nightstand, removed his glasses to neatly set them next to the base of the lamp and joined me in the bed. "I told her you stay with your girlfriend most nights, but you usually crash on the couch."

The surprise of it made my voice escalate in pitch and crack. "And she believes you?"

"I said she was hot. I never said she was smart." He giggled and kissed me goodnight.

The three of us worked out serious time management issues, but we didn't always get it right. One night Candice called while I was in bed watching television with Doug. After he ended the call, he told me I had to leave because she was coming over. He began frantically taking our photos down throughout the apartment to place them, face down, in the drawer.

"Doug, I am in my pajamas! Are you kicking me out of my own bed?" I shouted in horror.

"Hey, it's not like you haven't done it to me before! Less talky, more walky." He looked around to make sure he got every frame, handed me a pair of shorts then waved at me to hurry up.

Shamefully, he was right. I had claimed dibs on the apartment a few times before I met Patty but certainly never kicked him out of bed. As I stood to put the shorts on, he told me that Candice was less than ten minutes away, so he insisted that putting some purpose in my step was imperative. I grabbed some last minute items, reminded him repeatedly to change the sheets and walked to my car after calling him a bastard yet kissing him at the door.

Laughing in disbelief, I phoned Patty to tell her the story. She welcomed my unexpected request to stay the night; however, my curiosity waned heavy about this girl's appearance. Making the decision to wait was easy. Douglas always spoke highly of her body and beautiful red hair, so this opportunity to stalk my husband's fire crotch lover was not going to waste. Sitting in my car waiting for a glimpse of her was quick and painless. She practically pulled into an empty spot the moment my door shut. She put on a little lipstick in the car and walked to our front door. Before she knocked, she adjusted her skirt and flipped her red hair behind her shoulder. Douglas opened the door with a Cheshire cat smile. Candice disappeared into my apartment before the door closed. The bottom line was this; his girlfriend arrived, so his wife had to leave and spend the night with her girlfriend. Surreal life was my reality.

When Douglas wasn't seeing anyone, the reality of our marriage took him to a different place. He wasn't himself. His wife was seeing someone, going to the club too much, and drank more often than not. This was a far cry from the rock solid foundation of our first five years. One of his most tormented evenings came after he came home from a wonderful date.

He was very upset when he walked in the door. My state of mind was peaceful as I enjoyed a movie with my cherished dog curled on my lap. Cheerfully, I asked how his date went. Rather than the usual details and smiles, he seemed distant and lost.

He stood by the door with his keys in hand immobilized. He stared at me, blinked a lot and finally spoke. When he did, it was hushed and low like he felt somewhat guilty. "We went out to eat. She is really, really smart," he said and paused in thought for a long time before he carefully pulled off each shoe and aligned it against the nearest baseboard.

His demeanor was very unlike his usual post-date euphoria. "That's it? What else? Did you get some?" I smiled. Maybe I read him wrong.

He pushed a button on his very expensive Omega watch that released a clip. He shimmied his hand and carefully pulled the watch off. "We had intellectually stimulating conversation then

I took her dancing." He re-clasped the clip and set the watch on the counter between the living room and the kitchen. "We went back to her place and chilled on the couch with some drinks then watched a movie." A reminiscent smile gently peaked from his lips.

My brain assumed that it did not go well from the behavior he was presenting. But the smile threw me off. "So, did you have a good time? Did you do it? What's wrong with you?" My hand stroked the dog several times from his head all the way down his curled tail before Doug answered me. He was preoccupied with reliving the date in his mind. Physically he was in our apartment undressing, but he was definitely somewhere else.

Doug set his keys on the bar, two fingers away from the Omega and began to slowly unbutton his shirt. "Yes, we had sex. It was nice." His tone was melancholy.

"Nice? Honey, what is wrong with you?" My worry escalated even though I continued to sit on the couch and stroke my Shih Tzu.

There were moments when he seemed to make eye contact, but the rest of the time he stared at the dog or my shirt or the back of the couch. "She was a good kisser. She desired me and got hot for me. She made me feel like she wanted to be with me; needed me." He took his shirt off and hung it over his arm like a butler's towel.

"So, it was good then? Why are you acting so weird?"

"It was really good actually." He walked toward me, shirt hung from his forearm and sat on the coffee table at my feet. He seemed fascinated with how amazing the sex was as he retold the details. I listened while he explained how wet she became after her breathing changed and her entire body temperature went up. Her pupils dilated when she was aroused; those things, he said, you cannot fake. Those things were biological reactions to stimulation, and those things did not happen when we were in bed together.

There was a long pause. My fingers repetitiously combed through the dog's hair because I was nervous as to where he was going with this. Doug finally tilted his head, scrunched his eyebrows and said, "You really *don't* like having sex with me, do you?"

My hands immediately jerked to cover my open mouth. The tears filled my eyes in an instant because he wasn't blinded by love anymore; he finally understood. It didn't matter how many ways I explained my sexuality; it took another woman's affections for him to see the comparison. It was a reminder of how a man and a woman should behave in the bedroom. Biology provided tangible evidence to support my claims. For an agnostic man, it was proof positive.

I cried because the reality of it all was a painful truth for him to discover. I never meant to cause him this torment, but there it was sitting on our coffee table. How we ever fell to sleep with our shattered minds frankly eludes me, but we did. The realization of our seemingly flamboyant lifestyle was pushed aside for a time. We didn't know what to do with that information anyway. I'm sure we felt everything would just work itself out. So, Douglas continued schooling and dating. My life resumed with two relationships and college. I phased out stripping as mud wrestling became my main source of income. It actually paid better after honing my skills to become the champion.

To be clear, it was never a legit job. It was something fun for the tourists to volunteer doing with the added bonus of free drinks and money if you won. It was instant cash at the end of the night that I didn't have to claim on my taxes. For months, it literally brought in about 400 dollars a week.

The thing is, it was a show that looked very intense and real, but I knew when to lose too. Had I wrestled and took the entire pot of cash every time, the crowd would have caught on. My talent was so perfected I learned how to flip girls from a kneeling position making sure they landed safely, yet with just enough power to spray onlookers with a nice coat of mud. Because of my mad skills, I have been in the background of a few reality dating shows, but the true-life story behind the dirt is always deeper than it seems.

The three of us maintained what we felt was the best scenario for our lives so, yes, mud wrestling was how we paid the bills.

One evening the manager of the show called to ask if I was coming in to "work." She was worried because she only had three girls signed up. "Don't worry; I always come so I'll get you more wrestlers." That was when I began calling it my job.

Work began at 9:30 pm where I would start manipulating the crowd for recruits. This was not part of the routine but getting more girls to voluntarily wrestle was more money in my pocket. The night ended when the last girls showered then we all walked to the front of the casino for our payout. About six months after I began the casino earned such a huge profit, they began doing it two nights a week, which was only more money for me. Patty went with me and was the only non-wrestler allowed in the ready room other than the manager. She helped clean up the hotel room at the end of each night and provided assistance to the manager. It gave her a validating role, and she rather enjoyed hosing off the bikini-clad girls in the walkway between buildings.

She was always supportive of the crazy things I did, including margarita wrestling at a club, which was broadcast on pay-per-view. I lost after six minutes in the green water but was the quickest 375 bucks ever earned. A seven-hour day shift at the strip club might bring in that much.

Money was tight even with the National Guard income, so I entered myself into a karaoke contest in hopes of winning the thousand dollar prize. After I made it into the top ten finalists, Doug and Patty went with me to the taping of the finale, which was to be broadcast on a local television station.

It was a typical Vegas set-up with lights and a flamboyant host. Most of the contestants were strangers to each other. Each won their place at different karaoke nights across Las Vegas.

While waiting in the wings, I befriended Kim, a thick Italian girl with an exceptionally bold personality. She had huge brown eyes, a large white smile, and huge tits that were almost too big for her body. Her wit impressed me more than her beautiful voice, which nearly had me in tears. After her song, she suggested we get a drink at one of the many bars in the casino. We were there about an hour before I got a text message from Doug and Patty who wanted to wish me luck at intermission. They met us at the bar where we shared brief introductions before Kim, and I left for our losing results.

There wasn't another mention of Kim until I ran into her at karaoke night the next week. Patty opted to stay in that night, so I went alone. When Kim invited me to sit with her and a few friends my night was so much fun I had to tell Patty all about it.

After a year of absolute devotion to Patty, others found it hard to believe my level of faithfulness. We had our rare issues, but otherwise, we had a great relationship. I never wanted to be with other women. Given my scandalous history, Rayya and Joy were stunned with my loyalty especially since they thought she was the ugliest girl I had ever been with besides Lindsay; I mean "April."

I always defended Patty's beautiful green eyes and strawberry blonde hair. I doted endlessly over every freckle and dimple on her body. Her sense of humor was ingenious, and her passion for trying new things was a point I proudly emphasized. We were inseparable and had the most amazing adventurous sex, with heavy lovemaking overtones. We were solid – until she accused me of cheating on her with Kim.

The accusation caught me off guard. In my reality, other women didn't exist.

Did she see something developing that I did not? Doug and Patty fulfilled my every desire so being with Kim was absolutely unnecessary, but a week later, I found myself fully engulfed in the middle of a make-out session in the back of Kim's car. However, the guilt was as overwhelming as her passionate kisses. I felt terrible about each little pleasure and finally told her I shouldn't be there. She backed away from my face for a moment to ask, "Then why are you?"

It was that easy for me to realize my mistake and leave regardless of her protests.

Between Doug and Patty and the slow burn of self-discovery, my emotional state was beginning to unravel. Rivers of tears flowed in front of my friends that year. I cried on the phone to my step-mom about being gay. She told me that if I loved Douglas, I would let him go. My sister caught an earful of heartache and confusion every time she phoned. My mother pretended to understand until the actuality of my life was fully explained during a traffic jam on the Vegas strip. The conversation turned sour when she asked how Doug was doing and never asked about Patty, and then preached the Bible. She told me that I needed to start praying. This was the first time I ever scolded my mother and hung up on her. "Patty and I pray every night before we go to bed."

When she called back, I reluctantly answered but I was still in the standstill traffic jam so really, there was nothing else to do but talk through this.

"I have two relationships, Mom. I hate omitting half of my life. Do you know Patty and I studied for a week for her psychology exam, and she got a B? I am so proud of her. But you don't want to hear that. So, the next time you call and ask me anything, I'm just going to tell you that everything is fucking fine."

"You shouldn't be with a man and a woman. It isn't right."

"Well, what if I got divorced and was a lesbian?"

"No. That isn't right."

I raised my hand up and slammed it down onto the steering wheel. "So, the only answer is to leave Patty and be married and have babies."

"Yes."

"Mom. I love you, but I really can't continue this phone call. I am going to go now, okay." We hung up the phone in mutual frustration.

My inner turmoil was the dominating factor in my infidelity once again. As if my chaotic life wasn't messy enough, I found freedom in getting involved with a butch girl from my National Guard unit. In the same week that Zelda and I consummated our affair, I received a letter from my mother about living in sin and my hell-bound afterlife.

Mom wasn't the only one who couldn't wrap their mind around my life. On my weekly coffee gatherings, Joy and the rest of the gang consisting of two straight men, one straight girl, and four lesbians—all demanded details.

"Come on guys, of course, Doug knows," I defended myself as we sat at a table outside of the coffee establishment so we could chain smoke.

"How can you keep up?" Joy asked. Her labret sparkled under the plaza lights.

"Shit, I forgot you had a husband!" Troy lit another cigarette. "Where is Doug anyway? We liked him *way* better than Patty." He high fived the other guy at the table because they liked any straight male who joined coffee night. They joked that it was another pair of balls to counterweigh the estrogen at the table. Everyone laughed.

Then Ashley reminded the table of the mean shit she said to Patty the first and last time I invited her for coffee night. Specifically, after Patty joked about making me howl during sex and Ashley chimed in maliciously, "Joy made that discovery long before you came around honey. Tell us something we don't already know."

I was embarrassed all over again as I remembered the awkward intensity of the moment. "Come on guys; she is really not that bad." My defenses surfaced through my smile. "I love her freckles, and I think she is beautiful," I added with honesty.

"Is that what you tell Zelda?" Troy sarcastically chimed in to which Ashley high fived his non- smoking hand as everyone, all seven of them, laughed. Admittedly I shook my head and laughed too. I totally asked for that one.

As happy as my life was with Doug and Patty, it was utter nonsense to continue my affair with Zelda, but the sex kept me coming back for more. We didn't have much in common and, to be frank, any deep compatibility would have never been reached no matter how hard she tried. She couldn't compete with the levels of love I shared with them.

It was madness.

To further escalate the insanity of my scandalous life, Patty inadvertently exposed the secrets of my Soldier Show sexcapades to Douglas. While I was chatting to her online one night, Doug stood behind me as a way to passively tell me it was time for bed. There on the screen was the blinking cursor behind the last question Patty typed. *Does Doug know you cheated with that guy in the Soldier Show?*

"What guy? What did you do?" Doug asked. His face went pale. I said nothing because I was caught.

As my skeletons fell out of the closet, the arguing grew more intense while I sadly attempted to explain that it was simply a mistake, I made five years prior. There was no need to lie at that point so when he asked what else I had done I purged; divulging the fact that I prostituted myself once to a virgin as eloquently as possible. Without hesitation, he started packing a bag.

Through hysterical crying, my desperate words begged him not to go while snot dripped from my nose. My body grew tired from the hysterics and, eventually, it slumped to the floor in our bedroom as he paused from packing only to yell. "Give me one good fucking reason why I should stay!" His heart was beating so hard that I could almost see it through his chest. It looked as if he was about to burst as each pump created an unnatural motion forward.

From my slumped position on the floor, with tears in my eyes, I attempted to explain. "I'm in *love* with you, not them. I have made mistakes that I deeply regret." I tried to inhale, but the mucus and swelling on top of hyperventilation made it nearly impossible. My attempts to receive air made me choke. A pause to breathe was necessary for me to continue and to get a grip on the reality that surrounded me. "I don't even like men. I don't know why I did it. I will never be with another man in my life. I swear to you!" I began to calm myself more by sucking air into my lungs through my mouth as I wiped my swollen, snotty face. Finally, with controlled conviction, I added, "But I'm never leaving the women. Don't ask me to leave the women. I will understand if you can't handle that. I'm just so sorry Doug. So sorry."

His heart was absolutely broken, crushed before his very eyes with lies from a woman he vowed to love forever. He stood at the end of our bed with his clothing crammed into a bag, half of which was hanging out of the opening. In my feeble position on the opposite side of the bedroom, my knees pressed painfully into my chest; I waited for his reaction. A part of me fully expected a slap in the face as he walked out, but he was beyond disgusted and couldn't muster the energy to waste on touching me.

I slept on the couch for the next few days.

He stayed, obviously because he loved me, but in later months I learned of an indiscretion he'd had before our open marriage agreement. I suspect this is why he succeeded in letting my infidelity go although the pain of it never left. Throughout this adversity, Douglas and I resumed our marriage. The brutal truth of the matter was that we were both technically cheaters every day that we continued to have relationships with other people. Or was it? The way we saw it, all of the others were secondary.

Zelda was asking for drama in her life by being with me. She knew about everything but deeply hoped for a sincere chance at love. She didn't come from the best life and repeatedly explained how she only passed high school because she was the star athlete.

She also told me I was the only real lesbian she had ever been with, despite being married.

Part of Zelda's appeal was her resemblance to Doug. Visually, she was the female version of him, or so it seemed to me at the time. Only she was distinctly less educated. She had an athletic body and huge gravity-defying tits that she hid very well. They surprised me the first time her shirt hit the floor, and there was no bra holding them up.

It was definitely a physical thing with Zelda although I denied it when she asked. She didn't need my confirmation of her status as a piece of meat. That would have been mean.

Our sexual tension was chart-topping. It really got ridiculous on several occasions but especially when she surprised me at a seedy gay bar that Rayya found on the other side of town. It was the dirtiest, most run-down Hispanic shit-hole on the streets that tourists don't even know about and certainly wouldn't go to if they did. I was appreciative of the broken lights throughout the place. Had they worked, I would have actually seen the nastiness on the walls. Despite all of this, it was a refreshing change from our normal hang-out.

Rayya hit the dance floor as soon as we walked in. I sat on a chair in a dark corner, texting Zelda vulgar messages. Suddenly, the bitch plopped herself into the chair across from me. The smell of fresh shampoo and rum flew into my nose through the thick smoky air. The music beat hard as she slouched with widespread legs. "Surprised?" She said finally, after staring at me with smooth butch confidence. I was speechless for a moment, so she continued. "I'm horny; we should fuck." Her face was stone serious as she slid her hand into the front of her pants, called me over with a head nod and began rotating her hand and wrist. "Come over here."

"What, here? Right now?" I looked around with eyes as wide as saucers. It was dark but not dark enough to do it in a club full of people.

"Yes. Come over here and fuck me or I'll fuck myself." She unzipped her pants with her free hand and exposed much more than a hint of the goodies.

Who am I to deny a woman who is throwing herself at my feet? I immediately jumped on top of her as my fingers slid inside without effort. A few moans escaped her lips before Rayya stumbled over with two girls. Her tank top was sweaty and stretched out. Her button-down shirt, which she ironed repeatedly before we left her apartment, was thrown over her shoulder. She stood feet from me on top of Zelda with a drink in each hand. "Janell, I got us some drinks! What are you doing back here in the dark?"

"I'll be right there," I said, trying to act as if she only interrupted a simple make out session.

"Oh, hey Zelda," Rayya managed.

"Hey," Zelda said just like she would have done without my fingers deep inside of her.

Rayya headed back to the bar as she mumbled Dominican slang. We don't remember too much about the rest of the evening. The next day as I drove to visit Zelda, Rayya called to give me a piece of her mind over the night's events. "You are so nasty. What were you thinking?"

Giggling through a yawn, I explained it the best I could. "She just opened her pants and showed me snatch! What was I supposed to do?"

"Even worse. That's white trash. You are one crazy white bitch."

"You know she is like a quarter black or something."

"Oh, that makes it better. *Not!* Those girls wanted to meet you, and you ruined it!"

"I don't like feminine chicks; you know that Rayya."

"I know you like to steal tranny purses, don't get it twisted. Remember that? I ain't never seen a white girl snatch a bag that fast in my life."

"You had to bring that up. Now you know I was broke and hungry when I did that."

"We sure did eat good at Taco Meh-he-koe that night, didn't we?"

"Yes, we did, and I brought food home to Douglas."

"Don't get it twisted." We laughed so hard I nearly missed my turn.

"Well, I'm going to go; I'm almost at Zelda's."

"What are you doing there?"

"What do you think?"

"Crazy white bitch you are so nasty. Call me later."

"You know you love me. Bye Rayya."

We ended our call as I pulled into Zelda's apartment complex. It was a beautiful day in Las Vegas. The sun was bright and clear with a wonderful breeze that swept the heat from your skin.

Before my knock beat at her door, I checked my watch and noted the two hours I had before Patty expected me. These are the things a person does when they cheat – shamefully, always on a tight schedule.

Zelda quickly opened the door, and the second I saw her face. I knew I was going to get it. In my head, I repeated *oh shit* over and over. The seduction was oozing out of her pores; I could smell it. The second the door closed, I knew she was going to attack me in the foyer, so I dropped to the floor to pet the dog. It was the only thing I could do to prevent her from slamming me against the wall like I so desperately wanted. While I gave her dog some attention, she stood over me, waiting for that moment.

"I have to pee," I said and then stood. Our eyes met uncomfortably.

"Hi to you too."

As I passed Zelda, she brushed her full body against mine and put her face in my neck. For a second, I thought she was going to bite it, but she smelled my scent like it was intoxicating her. My legs went weak as the hairs on my back stood erect. I walked down the hall through her bedroom and gently closed the bathroom door. My head shook as I sat on her toilet. *Holy shit, I am totally getting fucked.* I buried my face in my hands and squeezed my skin with excitement. I composed myself, flushed, and gave myself a quick glance in the mirror. My smile was unforgettable. Scandalous.

It was a calculated, focused dash for the sink to wash my hands since Zelda was nowhere in sight. I lathered and rinsed them well since I knew something was about to go down. Pun intended. My toothbrush was in the holder next to hers, so I pulled it out and began brushing. That is when, through the reflection of the mirror, I caught an ominous figure standing in the doorway of the bedroom. I spit out the toothpaste and scooped water into my mouth to rinse. My face was practically in the sink as I swished it around, then spit a second time. When I lifted myself upright to wipe my face, Zelda grabbed my shoulders and spun me to the wall. She effortlessly removed my shirt and stripped me of my jeans before I could comprehend what was happening. We were savages for each other, but once her fingers began doing their magic, I succumbed to her whims.

She never gave me a chance to enjoy the calm after the storm. Normally, I'm a giggler after an orgasm, which can turn into full-blown loud laughter. There have been accusations of laughing at my partners in the finer moments of my sexual adventures, but it's just one of those fucked up things that happen to me, like my mother calling me Fungus or shitting my pants in a Wal-Mart parking lot. Twice.

However, Zelda wasn't playing games. Her sexual prowess was perfection. She grabbed my arm and seductively swung me into the opposite side of her room before my giggles could surface to audible sounds. My back made contact with the wall just before she flipped me around and nudged my head downward with her fingers. I willingly complied and pressed my cheek against the cold barrier to the apartment beyond. Her left arm wrapped around my waist as she pulled me close to her, which forced my body to bend a little.

As she pumped her fingers, my face slid down the wall while my hand inadvertently began slapping it. The louder I moaned, the harder I hit it. My legs progressively began to give out, so my body inched closer to the floor. We were practically on the carpet when she scooped me up with the arm still around my waist into a semi-standing position. It was like she somehow had super strength. It was so fluid and effortless. She demanded I stand up, but through heavy breaths, I told her I couldn't, so she continued to hold my weight as she fucked me.

When I came again, she slowly placed me on the floor where I sat Indian style with my forehead against the wall. I was limp, my face was numb, and I needed a moment to catch my breath.

"Are you all right?" she asked not knowing what to do.

"Uh huh." My hand frantically waved her away as if to give her permission to go ahead and do whatever. I pushed my finger up to signal to her that another minute was required. She waited on the bed. While I caught my breath, my crotch seethed with heat and felt uncomfortably stretched. It actually hurt and I flinched when I finally stood up. "I'm going to shower," I said with a dry mouth.

Zelda immediately jumped to fetch water from the kitchen and wash her hands. She was attentive like that. As I undressed and unclipped my watch, I noted the time. From the moment I checked my watch at the door, all of the events encompassing two orgasms were accomplished in 8 minutes! I'm talking about petting the dog, peeing, washing my hands, brushing my teeth and count them, *two* orgasms.

"You are shitting me," I accidentally spoke aloud as my hand stretched into the shower to monitor the temperature of the water. As I carefully stepped in, I thought, *that's what happens when you have deep sexual attraction and mad skills. This bitch is a pimp.*

Behind the privacy of her shower curtain, I soaped my hands to wash the painful abnormality that demanded attention between my legs. At the top of my vagina was a long protruding object that looked like a swollen construction workers thumb, jutting an inch beyond my outer lips.

Upon closer inspection, my mind reasoned with the worst possible scenarios that my melodramatic brain could produce. It must be a hernia tear… in my clit? Is that even possible? When I tried to touch the bulging tissue, the pain didn't register as pain but hyper-stimulation. Was this what happened when you had an orgasm? Would it go back to normal and how long would it take? How the fuck would I explain how I got a mini-dick to Doug?

When my quick but highly contemplative shower was over, I gingerly stepped into my clothes and sat carefully on the corner of the bed. Zelda obediently walked in with a glass of water and handed it to me. She had no idea that her charms were dismissed by my obsession with exploding vagina-parts that were uncomfortably pulsating in my pants. The only thing that pulled me from my thoughts was the ice clinking at the bottom of my glass. The sound triggered reality, clarity, and guilt. While quenching my insatiable thirst, I thought about how much I truly hated ice. My girlfriend would have never brought me a drink with ice.

In fact, she would have never done a lot of things that Zelda did. The obvious point here is that they are two different women, but one had my heart over the other. It takes more than a good roll in Las Vegas to win my jackpot.

Chapter 11

Douglas and I did not gamble. We barely had enough money to pay our bills most months. We certainly were not going to put a five dollar bill in a slot machine and hope for thousands let alone twenties like Zelda did.

When our finances continued to spiral downward, the gravity of our situation led us to consider moving in with Patty. She'd offered her four-bedroom home to us on many occasions for a small renter's fee and swore it would be best since we were all students with odd jobs. It was also more convenient for our type of relationship. We declined until the National Guard repeatedly denied my requests to enter Active duty and the first bill went unpaid.

When moving day came, Patty was ecstatic. She was enthusiastic as she helped Doug carry the heavier pieces into his new room across the hall from her master bedroom. Our prearranged designated days for each partner remained the same, so I technically did not have a room of my own. My clothing was dispersed between closets and drawers in both rooms. Doug shared a bathroom with another renter, and I used the one within the master suite.

At first, it was an odd transition to share the same home with my husband and my girlfriend. We walked on eggshells to respect personalities and the dynamics of my two relationships. It was difficult to establish private time and allow natural cultivation that happens when you have one partner with the other one around the corner. The last thing any of us wanted to do was hurt the others. Within the first few days, we realized we needed a routine to make the transition easier and lessen any awkward moments.

In a moment that could have gotten heated between me and Patty, Doug interrupted the beginning stages of a make-out session to see what was cooking for breakfast. We felt like we had been caught doing something naughty and stopped immediately.

"Morning honey," I said.

"Good morning, Doug," Patty said as she dunked her hands into the sink water to shamefully scrub dishes.

"Morning ladies! So, which one of you is cooking my breakfast?" Doug asked as he clapped his hands together and jutted his eyes back and forth between the two of us with a smile. It was a fantastic, ingenious way to fade the tension even if it meant directing negative attention right back at him. Patty and I immediately dove right into scolding him about being late for breakfast.

"Ha! You should have been down here earlier…"

"You know where the eggs are…"

"…just like a man…"

"We already ate…"

Then, when the jokes began to die down, Patty tried to recover him. "I got you, Doug. We both know Janell can't cook." Her redirection was perfect. They always teamed up when the opportunity presented itself. It was a small way to get back at me for making them share their time and love. Douglas laughed in agreement.

In the few days before we finally sat down to work out a cooking schedule, awkward moments were becoming plentiful. Once meal planning was organized, it helped pinpoint who was going to be in what room at a specific time. In essence, it helped limit the number of times we bumped into each other during private moments. Weeks later, we tried to make cooking something all three of us could do, but unless someone was working the grill, it was just too many chefs in the kitchen.

Food also gave Douglas and Patty an outlet for friendly competition. They created special meals to out-cook each other while I rocked the basic chicken dishes. The three of us would agree that we were eating the most healthy and dynamic meals on a daily basis. It was the contributing factor in the development of a hierarchy in our triadic unit. Well, we called it our family.

The only argument that ever came out of it was who ate the steak? I can still remember Doug laughing on the couch while Patty yelled into the freezer as she pushed frozen meat around, "I was going to use it in my fucking stew tomorrow, you *ass*hole!"

Once the food choreography was mastered, our living situation became a little easier. I spent most of my nights in Patty's master bedroom, which was bigger and more comfortable. The three of us occasionally watched movies in the living room together but for the most part, did our own thing. I had lots of sex with Patty but limited accounts with Doug. In fact, to my recollection, there were only two engagements. His new girlfriend satisfied him and spent the night a few times, so this wasn't a problem.

Then around December, things got a little too "over-the-top ménage a trois" for me. Douglas was innocently watching television in the living room while Patty and I were in her bedroom getting frisky. Nothing super special about that until she took the opportunity to tell me between kisses, "I think I want the cock." Verbiage she picked up from Doug's vulgar jokes.

I immediately turned to get our strap-on from the drawer when her hand reached from the bed to grab my arm. When it did, she stopped me from pulling it out. "No, I want a real one."

Naked by the headboard, I shook my head in confusion. My forehead scrunched so tightly; it was almost painful. "What do you mean?" I asked for clarity. It never dawned on me that she would ever ask to sleep with my husband.

"I've never had sex with a man before. I want to try a real one," Patty explained. "Do you think Doug would have sex with me?" she asked.

My jaw fell to my naked chest. "So, my butch lesbian girlfriend is asking to have sex with my husband? Fuckin' weird. I don't know; you ask him!" I demanded, completely dumbfounded.

"Can you ask him for me?" she begged and squeezed my arm tighter.

"No! This is sick. What do you want *me* to do? Hold your hand while he fucks you?" I half shouted.

"Yes."

"Oh my God, gross! Are you serious?"

She was completely serious. "Please, Janell." Then she shot me her infamous pitiful look, emphasizing her blazing green eyes. I was always a sucker when she did that.

I took this as a challenge to her request. Before I lost my nerve, I broke free from her grasp, stomped dramatically out of the bedroom and stood naked at the top of the stairs, "Doug, Patty wants to have sex with youuuu!"

Patty giggled from the bed. When I walked back into the room, I grabbed the sheets to pull them over her naked body. She looked at me funny but didn't say anything. I squatted on the floor between the computer chair and the headboard after putting a pair of boxer shorts on.

"Are you mad?" Patty asked in a whisper.

"A little. This is just fucking weird. You are gay," I said quietly.

"So are you."

That's when Douglas walked into the bedroom completely unaware of the request that was shouted from the top of the stairs. "What did you say?" He was eating something from a bowl. Whatever it was sounded wet and sloppy.

"Patty wants to have sex with a real penis. She's never had sex with a man before," I informed him from my crouched position.

He swallowed his food. "Really? So, what does that mean? You want *me* to be the penis?" he asked with an unbelieving wet laugh.

Patty shook her head in agreement. When he saw that we were not kidding he pointed his fork to me to ask. "What are you going to do?"

"I'm going to hold her hand," I said. He laughed harder before Patty snapped at him.

"It's not funny, Doug!" she shouted from the bed as she pulled the sheet higher to cover her exposed boob. "She's my moral support. I'm nervous, okay? I can't do this without her here. Do you want to do this or not?"

"Are you sure?" Doug placed the fork in his bowl and specifically asked Patty to clarify that this was, in fact, her request.

"Yes!" Patty and I chorused.

"Give me a second to get hard and get a condom," Without skipping a beat he turned and walked out of the room.

I leaned in to kiss Patty while Douglas prepared himself. We lost track of time until we heard Doug ask again if she was sure just before he mounted the bed.

She stopped kissing me to squeeze her eyes as tight as she could possibly get them while Doug entered her. He is not exactly your average man; he's a small anaconda, really. Patty's grip on my hand was so strong it was painful, but I didn't make it known. She opened her eyes to tell me she loved me as he began pumping, and then requested my kisses again. I obliged until she couldn't focus on my lips anymore and needed to shout in ecstasy. I crouched near the bed and literally held her hand until she had an orgasm.

While the two of them transcended in pleasure, I experienced rejection. It was my most prominent emotional response besides the exceptionally traumatizing circumstance. The pleasure he gave her should have been mine to give. I was confused more than jealous as to why this was what Patty wanted, although I never questioned it again.

When they finished, Patty was full of rave reviews over Doug's penis. She was rather amazed at how it felt in comparison to a dildo and immediately talked about purchasing a realistic toy, complete with mimicked veins and testicles as she cleaned herself.

Doug was exceptionally appreciative of the compliments. In a way, his manhood was validated by making a lesbian have an orgasm. "At least *some*body likes it," he said as he washed his dick off in the sink.

"You don't like it?" Patty asked me as she sat on the toilet to pee.

"I don't cum," I answered frankly.

"All right ladies, I'm going to watch my show. Glad I could help. Patty, congrats on your first dick-down." Doug ruffled her hair as his laugh escalated in pitch. He dodged Patty's attempt to slap him from her seated position and ran out of the room snickering.

"How can you *not* cum?" Patty asked in amazement as if this was the first time that she ever heard me mention any of this.

"I don't know. I don't even get wet."

Patty washed her hands and splashed her face with water. "I can't believe you don't cum. That was amazing. I mean, I prefer when you make me, but that was awesome."

"Okay Patty, Jesus." I walked over to the computer chair and spun it around so I could sit in it as I watched her.

"Are you mad? Not even once?"

"Not even once. I'm not mad, but my butch lesbian girlfriend just got the cock from my husband. I'm a little unnerved and totally grossed out." I said as I sat back and rocked in the chair.

"Shut up." She walked over to me and bent down, so her face was inches from mine. Her beautiful jade eyes looked into mine as she confessed, "Nobody can make me cum like you do baby. Our sex is amazing." Her kiss seemed to make the world I was in fade away. I sunk gently into the chair until we slowly pulled away from each other and continued on with our normally abnormal lives.

It was a month or more when Douglas and Patty left for their second trip to Hawaii. Their common interest in diving made for a perfect vacation between the two of them. My ideal vacation did not involve water sports or lying on beaches where people kick sand in my face. I am not a fan of sweat, sunburn, or babies shitting in hotel pools. So, we agreed that I would stay home to take care of our three dogs and two cats.

Both of them told me in separate private moments as we kissed goodbye that they wished they were going with me. I reminded them of my never-ending complaint list, which refocused them to have a good time. They were happy little buggers when I dropped them off at the airport. I was relieved to get a whole week to myself.

It was during this week, while painting the living room that I realized I didn't want to live this life anymore.

Although it was a small realization, it was just enough to have a conversation with Doug after they returned from Hawaii. I chose a random work out session to do it. It was as hot as it usually was in your typical Las Vegas morning, so conversation while running was short and to the point.

"Do you want to stay in Vegas?" I asked already winded.

"No," Doug answered quickly.

"I do. Do you want to have kids?"

"Yes."

"I don't. We really want different things in our marriage."

"What marriage? This isn't a marriage." He pointed to our first turn.

"You're right. What do we do?"

"I don't know."

"Johnson told me I'm going to computer school. I leave in December for six months."

He was used to the military life giving orders, but it is funny that in the middle of this very serious conversation he was mindful of how my girlfriend would react. "Patty will be pissed."

"I'll send her money for rent, so you don't have to worry."

"Thanks."

When we arrived at the house, Patty was in the kitchen cooking as Douglas, and I ransacked her space for ice, water, and food. She was genuinely upset when I broke the news, so I was thankful for Doug's help with the explanation. It seemed to go over better coming from his calm words. He always had a way with swaying a person one way or the other.

In fact, he must have done this magic word-voodoo on Patty while they were in Hawaii because she wasn't fixated on my upcoming training and quickly let it go. However, later that evening she began asking lots of questions about anal sex instead. I was nothing but shocked.

"What's wrong with you? Why do you keep bringing it up?" I asked after the sixth comment about the subject.

"Well Doug had this book, and it talks about anal orgasms and all kinds of stuff. I read it while we were there," as she spoke, she was hesitant and used a lot of broken voice inflections that were not natural in conversation.

From these reactions, the truth was exposed, but I accused and asked her anyway. "Oh my God, you let him poke you in the butt, didn't you?"

"Well, we were doing it, and since I was reading the book, I told him I wanted to try it."

I was flabbergasted. "You guys were doing it? How many times did you do it?"

"Twice, but once in the butt."

"You *did?* I can't believe you fell for getting the old butt-fuck!" A giggle fell out of my mouth.

"Shut up, Janell. I liked it, and I want you to do it to me."

"Fuck you in the butt? Whatever you want baby, I'm down. I got a two-hour shower rule when there is asshole play involved, just so you know."

"I'm clean." She defended.

"I'm just saying." I clarified.

As the holidays approached, the complexities of my relationships with Doug, Patty, and Zelda overlapped, which drove me deeper into the bottle. My typical "two drinks and a water" tab was a distant memory. My average drink request became two double shots of tequila before I hit the dance floor with a Long Island iced tea in tow.

I was on the edge of alcoholism when I reported to military school the day of my ninth anniversary with Doug.

Chapter 12

The National Guard wanted me to become a computer geek, and the school where I would train was in Georgia. Housing was billets designated for those who were retraining. The building was a twenty-minute walk to the barracks for soldiers fresh from basic training. A huge football field with a track around the perimeter separated the two areas of lodging. Faintly, if you listened hard enough, you could hear soldiers repeating a cadence of the drill sergeants from the back door where I used to smoke.

The computer geek material was a little too deep for my technically retarded brain to grasp. Switches and networking are the ultimate elusive bore, but it would pay my bills.

Although my responsibilities and obligations led me to Georgia, my priorities remained focused on the world of sexual discovery. The first thing I did when I found out we were released for weekends was locate the nearest gay bar. Determined to take advantage of freedom from the trio back home I kept limited communication with them. My weak cell phone signal aided as the reason not to call every day.

Being alone in a new place didn't bother me. My extroverted personality helped me make quick friends. My first weekend out, I met a lesbian soldier who drove me back to post after the club announced last call. She was nearly six feet tall with a medium build and curly jet black hair.

My standards for accepting meaningless sex were as follows: You like? I like. Let's poke. So, that is how we had our sexual fling in an apartment that was not hers. Days later, I waited for her to pick me up for an official date while on a phone call with Peter, a fellow student. In anticipation of her arrival, I watched her park and get out of a clunky, rusted mid-size sedan from my fourth-floor window.

"Peter, oh my god, she's here. What the fuck is she wearing? Holy shit, I'm going on a date with the Matrix! Have you seen that movie? This bitch has a black leather jacket down to her ankles, black leather boots, black sunglasses, and her hair is slicked back into a ponytail with… holy shit Peter, the back of her hair is gone, like the bottom three inches is shaved off! Well, not completely, it's like an inch long under the ponytail; what a twat!"

Peter mocked and pieced random quotes together from the movie. "Are you ready for the truth Neo; the green pill or the red one?"

Loud noises cut my laughter off. "I gotta go; I can hear her clod-hopping boots stomping up the stairs."

When Matrix knocked on my door, I tried to wipe the disappointed look from my face and open it with a genuine smile. She was respectfully greeted as I tried to think of the best way to mention her apparel. "Wow, I didn't know where we're going, and it seems that I am underdressed." I pointed to my graphic t-shirt and jeans.

She grabbed me in true butch form to pull me into her leather-covered arms. In an instant, the stink of cheap cologne swamped my senses. "Do not worry; this is the nicest jacket I have because I wanted to take you to a nice restaurant."

"Oh, do I need to change?" I looked down at my outfit. "I thought this would be casual and I didn't bring dressy stuff here to training."

"It is inside the mall; we can go shopping afterward."

In my head, the four-year-old version of me threw a temper tantrum. What nice restaurant could possibly be inside a mall and how could I act my way out of being embarrassed? The prospect of a free meal and possibly more sex made me seem gracious as I grabbed my jacket and bit my lip.

Politely, she escorted me to the car with utmost respect and made sure I was seated comfortably before she gently closed my door. She played music at the opposite ends of the spectrum to be accommodating. Other than the Queen of the Dammed wardrobe, she was doing everything right.

We pulled into the mall with bass so loud it shook the rear view mirror. If that wasn't enough to grab common folk interest, her stereotypical vampire attire most certainly pulled them in. To fuel the stares from other patrons, she was overwhelmingly polite. She opened every door, guided me through them, ensured I walked first and pulled my chair out. She was the perfect respectable gentleman.

The way she carried herself was reminiscent of proper wealthy kinsmen of the 1800s, always one step ahead of her fair lady's needs. Her control was intimidating with an undeniable sensitivity. In her long leather jacket, she seemed to glide across the mall tiles as if she was, in fact, undead. Her humanity became evident when she removed the jacket to expose a thick rainbow bracelet that tugged at the sleeve. It matched a colorful, handcrafted necklace, and one gaudy earring.

That is when I noticed her fingers were adorned with oversized gothic metal rings which shimmered as she handed me an opened menu. She was irrefutably visually interesting to look at and embarrassing to be associated with. I deeply questioned whether a free steak and sex was worth all of the appalled looks.

To her credit, it was a decent restaurant; low lights, a water feature, good music playing overhead. Just as I began to relax and enjoy myself things took a twisted turn when she suddenly divulged that she moonlit as a dominatrix for two faithful customers. This may or may not be winning first date conversation, but she used big words, so the impression I got was that of an intelligent, independent, albeit slightly socially inept woman. Matrix was definitely unique. There were a million questions to ask, but she was very patient. The first one, of course, was about sex. "No, I do not have sex with them. They are into humiliation. I verbally disrespect them, make them lick my boots, and step on their testicles. The usual."

"I did that to a guy at the strip club! He paid me forty bucks for six minutes. It's nuts. Ha! Get it?" I laughed, but she smiled graciously.

"Yes, it is crazy. I think you would make a fantastic dominatrix. I can see you doing very well within the subculture."

"I don't think I could do it for a living. I mean, I dated this girl once and really laid into her. She said her jaw was tight for two days. But that was because I loved her. I couldn't do that with anyone I didn't love, respect, and trust. I mean, I swear to you that she had an emotional orgasm if that makes any sense. She cried a deep, pleasurable, transcending cry, you know? I've never heard anything like that before."

"Perfect sense. That is what I do. Sadomasochism is not solely about physical pain. I knew you were a "Dom" when I met you. You are a strong woman." Matrix smiled.

I must admit, the conversation boosted my self-confidence and got me thinking about the possibilities of opening many sexual doors. No wonder men paid her to break them down. She somehow allowed them to rebuild themselves in a different kind of way. This is the power of the dominatrix, not the leather. Lesson learned.

As eye-opening as our discussion was, I simply forgot about Matrix by the time the weekend arrived. In fact, I had no plans to ever speak to her again. Although interesting, she was a little too… Matrix for my taste.

Charlene and I met on karaoke night at the gay bar which was more my style. She was an older lesbian who was probably a hot mullet-wearing dyke in the eighties. But as she sat at the bar enjoying a drink and listening to people sing, she initially seemed worn down. Life had happened to her, and from the looks of things, it had not been kind. Strangely, when she turned in the light of the bar her face morphed between tired hag and sexy older lady. Similar to those cars with opal exterior paint—one minute they are blue, the next green. To be perfectly honest no one could tell if she was pretty or ugly. At the end of the evening, my conclusion was undetermined.

Either way, her personality was vivacious and warm. She was an upbeat woman, unafraid to shake her ass on the dance floor. We became beer friends because Charlene was freaking awesome. We slept together because we were freaking drunk.

Charlene rented a room from another older conservative lesbian who frequently entertained her very young girlfriend from time to time. The younger girl was also a soldier on the same installation, so the four of us soon started hanging out.

My twenty-eighth birthday was around the corner. We were making plans for a huge gay party—until I got arrested for stealing. Only the Lord himself knows what possessed me to take that pendant with eighty dollars in my pocket, but I thought four years of financial struggle in Las Vegas was blameworthy.

Part of the required procedure for prosecuting soldiers charged with theft is mandatory counseling. During my first session, the psychiatrist told me it was a mid-life crisis after asking my age. He claimed he was writing a book about it.

"Are you also dating women?" he asked frankly with a pen in his hand ready to write my answer down.

"Excuse me?"

He looked to me to explain with a crooked smile. "The demographic for my book is women between the ages of 25 and 35. They seem to go through a mid-life crisis between these ages and do things they wouldn't normally do. Like sleep with other women. You are married, right? And are you sleeping with women?" His hand and pen went back to the paper in preparation.

"I'm open. Listen, what does this have to do with determining my mental stability and punishment? Am I getting kicked out of school or not?"

He diverted. "Would you answer some questions for me? For the book, of course."

I answered three or four questions before the pervert meter reached maximum capacity and I refused further queries into my sex life. His evaluation rendered a demotion one week before my upcoming promotion. I received extra duty and was restricted to my room in the barracks on my birthday.

It was embarrassing to tell Douglas and Patty later that evening. They offered words of encouragement and tough love to get my shit together. My arrest was briefly mentioned to Zelda, but she could have cared less; she was too excited to tell me how much money she won at the tables. She made arrangements to fly to Georgia for a visit and promised she would make up for my missing birthday party.

Ironically, Matrix called the day of my birthday to wish me a happy one, which was nice of her and much appreciated but it made me very uncomfortable. "How did you know it was my birthday?" I questioned.

"You told me when we spoke of horoscopes."

"You remembered that?" Admittedly, I was impressed but not enough to involve myself with her again.

"So, you got into trouble? Well how about this, I will stop by, and we will have a little mini party in the day room. I will bring the cake. It's not a problem at all."

God bless her beautiful face, she drove to the barracks within an hour, complete with a meal from Arby's, a card, birthday cake, and candles. It was sweet but a bit peculiar to share my special day with her and strangers in a community room. Every passerby was staring at the light from the candles in the top bun of the burgers and Matrix in her faux jacket and half shaved head. We must have been quite a spectacle. She did not stay long, but when she left, I watched her drive away from the window in my room. As my nose pressed against the cold glass, my breath fogged the pane, "You are nice but please don't call again. Fucking weirdo."

Although my infatuation with Zelda dominated most of my thoughts, there was interest in a young student from my class. She was nerdy, blonde, butch, and fresh out of basic training. Peter teased relentlessly, calling her a "baby dyke" and poked fun of my reaction to her as she walked into the classroom. My advances were ill spent. She was clueless to my attraction. When finally released from restriction, I bluntly asked little Private

Marche to go to the bowling alley with me. She accepted my offer as her face flushed and she nervously pushed up her glasses.

Most of the students frequented the bowling alley because drinking was legal for eighteen and up. Marche was a month from her twenty-first birthday. Inside the alley, in a separate room was a bar complete with pool tables, a back patio and volleyball pit. We shared a wonderful evening even though one of her scandalous friends begged me to fuck her behind a fence surrounding the volleyball court.

After last call, Marche and I stumbled back to our barracks completely drunk. We stopped midway behind a dark building so she could release the fluid in her bladder. She was youthful, full of energy and seemingly care-free, but she was a bit of a wallflower; socially reserved, if you will, until you made her comfortable. Part of my drunken conversation on our long walk was about my attraction to women who were confident and bold. She listened intently as we staggered home.

As our night came to an end, our paths, quite literally, divided. We found ourselves standing under an intensely lit streetlamp that seemed to be the brightest one on the road. It lit the intersection of a four-way stop where we said our goodbyes. This was where we prepared to split directions to our designated barracks. I headed left, she turned right. However, just as my first step hit the road, she grabbed my arm, spun me around and kissed me for all to see. Right there on a well-lit corner of a military installation.

She backed away with the biggest smile. "Text me. I have to run, seriously. Text me!" She ran toward the football field a little faster than normal because she knew I was watching.

Once comfortably tucked into bed, we began our onslaught of text messages. She explained how she cut her leg jumping

Unashamed

through the window of her room in an effort to elude the drill sergeants. Completely charmed, I found myself giggling out loud in the dark.

We shared sexual fantasies before I invited her to spend the night the next evening. Ramifications of a new student caught sleeping in my barracks were severe, not to mention we were both girls. What I asked of her was deeply rebellious and wrong on so many levels, but she walked to my room the next evening with her book bag and computer, fully prepared for a sleepover.

During a dry hump session, it was clear that there was an experience gap between the two of us. You see, she came into my world after my discovering interest in rougher sexual encounters. Everything Private Marche knew how to do was simplistic, soft and sensual. Though a pleasant, refreshing change, it bored me a little.

Twenty minutes into heavy petting, this little harlot had to remind her fledgling that clothing was optional. A seven-year gap in age can sometimes put clarity on experience differences. Case in point, the older, more mature Charlene wanted me to explore her vibrator collection within the first five minutes of our encounter. She didn't think anything of it, while I felt like a vibrator Nazi. But I digress.

Age aside, Marche was simply inexperienced, so I couldn't be mad at her as long as she was willing to try new things. If I could hold a vibrator to a clit, Marche could hold my neck to the wall.

Philandering with and training Marche distracted me from the trio who held down the fort in Las Vegas. Their phone calls became nuisances as I tried to find whatever it was that kept me searching. It seemed I wanted freedom to be gay on my own terms. Not Doug's, not Patty's, and certainly not Zelda's. All three of them had ideas of who they thought I should become.

Marche had none. She accepted me for the lesbian she thought I already was. Truth be told, booze and women numbed me from those complexities. It's the easy way to be out of the closet without actually going through the drama and heartbreak, and it was delightful for a change.

Being around inexperienced Marche and all her sweetness was definitely pleasant, like an easy listening station or pleasant like the mellow Christopher Cross song, "Sailing." If someone was in the middle of a full-on, red-eyed road rage war and "Sailing" suddenly began to play, who wouldn't fucking pause to sing the words? That's the effect she had on my life.

Charlene, although older, was closer to the craziness my life was accustomed to. When she invited me to the club with her roommates, Kathrin and Jill, I immediately accepted. A night out with the girls was required to be carefree.

Jill picked me up since she was a fellow soldier who lived around the corner from my barracks. We stopped for gas outside the installation and broke the ice on the drive to Kathrin's house. The minute we walked in the door I realized my phone was forgotten in the gas station bathroom. We returned to retrieve it adding an hour to our trip.

I was overly apologetic as we made the trek back to the house for a second time. She was a dull conversationalist with moments of humorous sarcasm, enough to keep me mildly entertained. The most interesting subject of our forced conversation was her occupation.

"A lesbian chaplain assistant, wow, how does that work for you?" I asked.

"I still have a life. I'm not the preacher or minister; I'm the assistant."

"Amen, honey."

Jill was a thin girl with short, dark brown hair, reminiscent of Rachel, only 30 pounds lighter. She had a very pretty face much like the description of Snow White in childhood fairy tales. If I was attracted to feminine women, she would probably be a good catch, but there was no chemistry.

Guilt and an undeniable voice challenged my attraction to fat butch women. Doug and Rico were heckling me from somewhere deep within my brain, so I forced myself to make flirtatious sideways glances. It was torture.

Once we arrived at Kathrin's house, I was excited to get the party started and remove myself from Jill's returned flirtation. I rushed from the frigid February night through the front door, displaying my rescued phone. With a huge relieved smile on my face, I presumed a cheerleading pose, complete with wiggling spirit fingers, yelling like a teenager, "I've got it!"

My eyes immediately locked on two unfamiliar faces standing at the back of the room holding pool sticks. The bigger girl had shoulder length brown hair and beautiful piercing eyes that widened when she saw me. Charlene straightened from the shot she was about to take at the pool table. She asked where I found it but as she spoke her words became gibberish as I was fixated on the butch girl. She too was entranced as she nudged the other lesbian without discretion and without breaking eye contact with me.

"Um, it was in the bathroom and uh the manager found it. How lucky was that?" I stumbled through the words.

Kathrin walked to me with a glass of red liquid. "You got to catch up girl, we've been pre-gaming it for an hour." I swallowed the delicious unknown contents, and everyone clapped in unison.

Charlene was the first to offer introductions. "This is Mandy and Rhonda; we met them last weekend and invited them out. The more, the merrier."

I can't remember if I shook Mandy's hand or stared into her eyes.

Regardless, the group wasted no time rushing to the cars. Mandy did not hesitate to assert that my seat was reserved in her vehicle. Charlene sat next to me while Rhonda perched herself in the front passenger chair. The ride to the club was full of tear-inducing laughter that had each of us claiming we were going to pee our pants. The three of them spoke with deep southern accents, which at times threw me into hysterics. My vibrant personality and quick wit kept them on edge. Between knee-slapping jokes, we either caught our breath or inhaled cigarettes as Mandy intensely stared at me through the rear view mirror. I didn't say anything.

Once we arrived, our club experience was full of dancing, wild lights, drag queen shows, cigarettes, and alcohol. Everyone had an exceptionally good time except Jill and Rhonda who were semi-locked into sitting at a table for most of the night. Lord knows we tried to get them onto the dance floor, but they were cemented, minus one or two songs they just couldn't refuse.

Toward the end of our evening, we met a couple who had announced their engagement. The feminine one put on a glittery tiara that said "Bride" as her attractive butch partner lit a cigar. Everyone celebrated their engagement until the bartender flicked the lights signaling imminent closing.

As club goers exited, our group of six became eight. We assembled our little clique in the parking lot while Kathrin concluded that we were all starving and had to get something to eat. I shivered uncontrollably while chatting with the bride. At that point, fuck food; I wanted to be warm.

The bride, feeling left out of the important restaurant decision-making process, turned from our conversation to vote, holding her partner's hand. When she moved forward, it pulled her partner right in front of me, uncomfortably close. So close, in fact, we could have leaned forward to kiss. They were still holding hands when the butch girl boldly flirted. "Whoa, hello, what's your name again? You *are* going to eat with us, right?"

"Um, I'm not really hungry, I'm sort of col—"

Her breath was loaded with liquor as she stopped me. "Listen, I *want you* to come." She grabbed my arm with her free hand and glared deeply with an agenda in her eyes. Her grip tightened on my skin.

Before I could answer, Mandy grabbed my free arm. "She can ride with me."

"I'm not really hungry. I don't want food; I want a jacket!" I said in a loud last-ditch effort to be heard as if my shivering wasn't noticeable.

"Well, let's get you in the car, and I'll turn the heat on." Mandy comforted.

"I don't want to go, Mandy; I need a jacket. This shirt is paper thin, guys; I'm really freezing." I said, as Mandy squeezed my left hand and the butch girl continued to tightly grip my right. Between them I stood, crucified.

"I'll take you to my place to get a jacket. I just live ten minutes away. We will meet you there, guys. I'm taking her to get a warmer shirt," Mandy said to the crowd.

The butch girl continued to stare at me with my arm in her hand. "You *have* to be there. You *have* to come." As Mandy pulled me away the girl reluctantly let go while shouting, "You'll meet us there, right? You'll be there, right?" Her bride tugged her in the direction the group was moving, oblivious to everything.

In the car, Mandy and I discussed the evening as she drove to her rental home. She was gracious enough to let me smoke in her new car.

"...right in front of her fucking wife! Can you believe that?" I said astonished.

"Girl, that is crazy! I didn't know she was going that far! I just rescued you because I saw her with a vice grip on your arm. You did not look happy, girl." Mandy giggled.

We pulled into a luxury home complex thirty minutes later; shame on her for lying to get me alone. The complex completely impressed me on every level although I knew it wasn't hers.

She unlocked the front door and held it for me to walk through. The second she shut the door I attacked her with ravenous desire. Our first kiss involved the acrobatic process of taking clothes off while shuffling back to the bedroom. We never made it to any restaurant. When we finally woke up, Rhonda was seated on the couch watching television. She threw her head back to shout down the hall. "Ya'll had fun, I heard. I knew you weren't coming back Mandy; you could have told me."

"Hey girl, I planned to come back, but I got attacked," Mandy said with a smile as she chuckled and walked to the kitchen.

I stood in the hallway yawning, in Mandy's shirt with my arms folded over my chest. It seemed to me that Rhonda's tone carried a hint of jealousy. I stood there for a minute pretending to watch whatever Rhonda had on the television then headed back to the bedroom. Mandy followed me to the bedroom with a glass of water. Again, we had ridiculously insane sex, which drove Rhonda out of the house sometime after the first half hour.

Mandy and I saw each other regularly for about two weeks, but marathon sex had to stop after twice missing morning formation. While soldiers walked past her car like zombies, my dumb ass ran to my barracks room to change out of club clothes.

Sex was amazing; however, the best thing that happened between us was friendship. As clueless as I am to the thing that unites two people, I'm even more oblivious to the thing that divides. During our short time as a couple, our relationship grew from whatever it was into a meaningful friendship. As connected as we were together, it wasn't in the cards, and although we tried, we never understood why. My guess is that one conversation, in particular, may have gently nudged us into the friend zone for good. It was in her car after Mandy picked me up for a sushi date. She commented on how upset I looked. She pried a little further when I tried to deflect her concern, and I lost my composure almost immediately. I sobbed about going through some serious shit that she wouldn't understand.

"Just tell me. What is going on?" Mandy begged and placed her hand on my thigh.

"Please don't hate me when I tell you this, okay."

She removed her hand from my thigh and folded her hands in her lap. "All right, I won't. What is it?"

"I'm gay, but I am married. Then, there is my girlfriend, and we all live together back in Vegas. I love them but I can't do this anymore, and it's fuckin' me up." An explosion of words and emotions poured out of me as I slobbered my way through the story.

She listened to every mumbled word and pieced together every hyperventilated sentence before she offered her thoughts.

"Ya'll are not the only people in the world. I was with my boyfriend, off and on, for eight years girl. We tried to do the same thing. He let me have girlfriends and everything. I loved him, I'm... still in love with him but I can't because I am gay. It broke his heart, girl, and he asked me to marry him, said he would live like that as long as I was in his life. And... well... that isn't right. It ain't right to be with a person if you can't be with them one hundred percent. So, I know. I know exactly what you are going through, believe me. The only difference is, we were never married, but we might as well have been."

While repeatedly wiping my eyes free of tears, she comforted me with details and parallels of her previous relationship. "I tried. We tried. My family loves him, I mean..." She trailed off into a private thought of her own before snapping back.

"I cannot suck dick to save my life, girl; it makes me want to vomit." She pressed her hand to her throat and made a gagging noise after emphasizing the 't' at the end of the word. I laughed so hard a snot bubble popped out of my nose. "You think I'm joking; it got to the point where dick grossed me out so bad, I got physically sick to my stomach when we had sex. *Phiz-ick-ally* sick. Like, puke in my mouth... Oh, dear God... I'm gonna throw up just thinking about it." She took a breath and swallowed hard. Then she fanned her watering eyes. With the other hand, she rolled down her window.

"Ya'll are just like me and him." She grabbed the top of her shirt and began tugging at it to create a breeze. "Girl, it ain't right to love somebody and feel like that."

My laughter at the puke comment subsided as I shook my head in total concurrence. It was as if she was preaching the Bible and the Holy Spirit was settling in on me. A calmness swept over my soul because on the deepest level; she didn't just understand; she knew my intense pain.

Our sexual relationship faded after that conversation, and instantly we became platonic.

Within the week, Charlene asked for my company. We too had become friends, but I'm sure she still had hope of another sexual experience minus the drunken fall we took out of the shower and the hangover that followed.

She drove me to a gas station with a donut shop built within the service area. We sat at a back corner table with our pastries and coffee to chat. She asked what was going on with Mandy, how I came to Georgia, how Doug and Patty became part of my life, and how I handled things back home.

Whatever she wanted to know was explained to include my version of falling out of the shower. We chuckled about the sound of the curtain ripping from the rod and how the shampoos and soaps went flying across the bathroom. Charlene's laugh was hearty and loud, but I loved making her cackle because it threw me into hysterics. She was good for my soul.

The next thing you know the coffee kicked in, and we were on a caffeine high. My objective was to make her piss in her pants with stories that make you want to slap your mamma.

"So, this couple must have been wealthy because they gave us fake names but who cares, right? They were so fucking rich I nearly shit my pants when Doug and I walked into their house. There were big game heads mounted high into the cathedral ceilings. I'm not talking about five; I'm guessing about thirty! Girl, it was like moose heads and wild boar and shit!"

"Where was Patty?" she asked to get the story straight.

"I don't think I was with her yet. Anyway, we are in the Jacuzzi, which by the way was connected to a pool that had a waterfall, and the husband starts kissing up on Doug."

"Wait, he *is* straight right?" she interjected. She held the coffee cup to her mouth, but she was too involved in the story to actually take a sip.

"Totally. And you should have seen the look on his poor face. So, me and the dude's wife, a hot redheaded totally fuckable mom, rush over to rescue him, and we start having a foursome in the Jacuzzi. Then the wife says we should take this to the bedroom, so we go back into the mansion and start doing it. Imagine: the wife sits on Doug's face, the husband starts sucking him off, and I'm bored like a motherfucker, so I participate as little as possible by giving the burly husband a hand job."

"No, you did not!" Her eyes widened with the steaming coffee cup still in front of her face.

"Yes, girl. They were rich, and we were hoping to get something out of it, shit. So, Douglas gets a little overzealous and bites the chick's clit too hard..."

"Oh shit! I fucking hate that!" She set the cup down on the table and sat back in her chair with a grimace.

"I know right. So, I rush over, start eating her out and make her cum. Then I'm like, fuck, how do I get out of this? I don't want to continue. So, I told the motherfuckers I started my period. Nobody was banging me that night."

Charlene laughed and refilled our coffee cups. "You are crazy."

"Char, it gets worse. The couple wanted to see us again. They told Doug that they wanted to find another couple to take to Africa for a month to go big game hunting. Let me break this shit down, an all-expense-paid thirty-day vacation... Vay-cay-shon, you hear me? To mother fuckin' Af-ree-ka!"

"Are you serious?"

"As a heart attack. But I had to work that night, so Doug went alone. He was so scared. He didn't want to go without me, and I had to convince him that it would be all right because the wife would be there. 'Just focus on her,' I told him. Then Doug says to me, 'What if the husband tries to suck my dick again?' With hands on my hips I yelled, 'Bitch, you better do it for Africa!'"

Charlene roared with laughter. Her knee hit the bottom of the little café table and practically knocked two cups of hot coffee to the floor.

"I was chanting that shit like a mantra, 'Af-ree-ka. Af-ree-ka.' I was trying to convince my husband to lose his dignity for twenty fucking minutes so we could go on a vacation to the motherland." I made random clicking noises and stood up to throw an imaginary spear.

"Holy shit! Did you go?"

"Do you see a bone in a bitch's nose and a tan on my face? Hell no, we didn't go! They fucking tricked him! When he got to the house, the wife left claiming she forgot she had an appointment."

"Oh my God, so he was left alone with the burly guy?"

"Yes, and of course, he got noodle dick and couldn't do it. The poor baby, he said he tried to let the guy suck him off for Africa, but he couldn't do it. I mean, he is straight, but he gave it the good old college try, God bless his heart." I giggled as I reminisced.

"I can't even imagine what was going through his mind."

"I know right. I don't blame him; the guy was hairy and kind of fat. I wouldn't want to have a first-time gay experience with a dude like that. He told me it was like having a hairy gorilla on his noodle dick." Both of us roared in laughter before getting up to take a piss break.

Charlene intensively listened to every word that came out of my mouth in the corner of that gas station. We were there for hours. She laughed at every detail I sensationalized, as most storytellers do, while we continued to fill our cups with more caffeine. As the stories continued, she became more amazed with my life.

"You crushed the man's balls with your stripper shoe? I can't believe he gave you forty bucks for that." The lights above the gas pumps automatically turned on as the sun began to set. The customers came and went. The day cashier clocked out as a new one rang up the next customer.

"She left you at the bar and took the pizza! How the hell did she drive drunk on a motorcycle and carry the god dammed box?" A fresh pot of coffee brewed at the drink station while a man outside smoked a pipe just beyond the window where Charlene sat.

"… Home invasions and prostitution, man, you sure do have some stories." A mother pushed her stroller into the ladies' room while two other women sat at a table behind me to eat a donut. Neither woman should have indulged.

"How did you get the tranny's purse out of the bar without anyone noticing? Wait, was that the same place Zelda threw her pussy at you?" A group of kids, who were too young to smoke, lit cigarettes near their car. An older customer walked over to yell at them for smoking near the pumps. Then he walked to the register to yell at the clerk for not paying attention. The cashier was apologetic, and when the gentleman left, she wrote and posted a sign that reminded patrons to not smoke near the pumps. Then she busied herself with cleaning the drink station for the fifth time.

"You should write a book."

"Huh? Oh yeah, Doug tells me that shit all the time." I looked away from the cashier spraying cleaner on the counter to my coffee, which Charlene refilled.

"No really, have you ever thought about it? You have some crazy stories, girl."

"I joke about writing one all the time but come on, who wants to read about the shit I've done?" I ripped open two sugar packets and dumped the contents into my cup.

"I'd buy it. You know we've been here for almost six hours? I have been dying laughing this whole time... I'd buy your book. You should write it. Make sure you write how the shampoo bottle flew across that bathroom!" Charlene could barely contain herself; she giggled through her words before she finished the sentence. I laughed when recalling our shared memory.

"Well, it gets worse. I got fucked up shit that I haven't even told you yet. Complicated shit that I couldn't imagine writing about... did I tell you I boned Jill?" I interrupted myself.

"No, you did not. What happened?" Charlene snapped.

"If I put this fucking story in the book, I'll have a chaplain's assistant putting a bounty on my head." I stirred creamer into my cup.

Charlene sipped her coffee and tightened her face when she realized there wasn't enough sugar in it. "She is uptight. Frigid in the bedroom, that's what Kathrin told me." She opened another packet of sugar, dumped it in and retested it to verify it tasted right.

"She was right, stiff as a board. Had her legs straight as an arrow, but that isn't all. Put it this way, lizard tongue kisses of which I couldn't get the onion taste out of my mouth for three days and an Amazon deep jungle bush that queefed during the entire sexual experience!"

Charlene threw her head back in half shock, half laughter, "Oh, are you shitting me?"

"That's what the fuck I said! The whole… time! How can you not feel that? My hair was puffing away from my face every fifteen seconds."

"Oh, Jesus. Well, Jill and Kathrin aren't serious, but I won't say anything… as long as you put it in the book." Her face lit up as she smiled from ear to ear. "Come on Janell, do it for Africa!" Both of us roared as patrons of the donut shop turned to see what the commotion was about.

Embarrassed, we finally removed our crumpled mound of sugar packets from the table and called it a night. As Charlene drove me back to the barracks, my mind raced over the profound idea that I could potentially help others by telling my fucked up life stories.

Figuring out my sexual identity was not an easy journey and surely through the laughter of my adventures someone could relate and benefit. Someone once told me that if it walks like a duck and it quacks like a duck, it must be a fucking duck. This was my holy shit moment. It gave me the confirmation I needed to come out of the closet for the third time.

Chapter 13

Strangely empowered with both confidence and clarity, I called each family member to tell them that I was a Lesbian. I paced alone outside of the barracks at Fort Gordon, Georgia as the phone rang. "I wanted you to hear it from the horse's mouth, Dad," I said as I lit a cigarette and paced the sidewalk surrounding the barracks.

"You're not telling me anything I didn't already know, Janell. You are more worried about it than I am," he professed calmly.

My mother was a little less accepting. "Are you sure? It's not right, Janell. It's a sin," she said and cried.

My grandparents on both sides were in their late seventies at the time and took it surprisingly well. The reason this was surprising was that my mother's gene pool is rich with numerous active evangelists or ministers of the word of God. In fact, my maternal grandfather was a retired Pentecostal preacher when I made that coming out phone call and my aunt was an active minister.

My grandfather, whom I deeply respect on many levels, reminded me, "You know the Bible and what it says. I am not the judge. The Father is. I still love you."

When I was finished coming out to everyone, I called my sister. After I'd told her their general reactions, she asked, "Did you tell Doug yet?"

"Well, he knows, I'm sure, but I have not officially come out of the closet to him. God, I haven't figured that part out yet. This was kind of spur of the moment."

"Wow. I can't believe you just called everyone out of the blue like that."

"It's not out of the blue for me. I've been dealing with this for years, you know."

"I know. Are you okay?"

"I'm good, just tired. Well, to be honest, I'm not sure how I feel right now. I think I just want to chill."

"Well call me back if you need to talk."

I hung up the cell phone and continued to pace while I smoked another cigarette. It was late, and the streetlamps attracted swarms of bugs. I watched them swirl and bounce around each other completely disoriented.

I couldn't relax. My thoughts circled my head like the moths in the light. I finally sat on the curb to smoke one cigarette after the other as I shut off my phone and didn't get up until my throat hurt from smoking too much. Eventually, I went to bed tormented between deep thoughts and numbness.

The next day I called Mandy after classes. "I came out of the closet to my family last night. I've done it now. There is no turning back at this point, Mandeesa. How did you come out?" I asked.

"I never did really. I just dated women. My family never asked either. I don't have a coming out story, girl."

"Well, I have like, three of them, and they all suck. Technically four, if you count when I hung up on my mom. You can have one of mine."

We said our goodbyes and ended the call.

Unashamed

My search for something to write on began the moment we ended the call. It was time to tell my story.

An unused yellow legal pad and a pen that only worked half the time appeared out of feverish searching. My first written line was an attempt at being a smart ass: *Ode to the mighty dry hump; the godsend to any little girl's clitoral repertoire.*

About twelve handwritten pages into the story, Zelda phoned. I had to step outside to get reception. "I am going to write a book," I told her.

"About what?" Zelda asked.

"My life. Check this out. This is the first line." I read it to her and waited for a response, you know a giggle or something, anything.

"What the hell does that mean?" Her self-proclaimed lack of education was apparent.

She once yelled at me when I said I was "humble" about my artwork. She screamed at me to get off my high horse and called me vain. I tried to explain what the word meant, but she yelled even harder for treating her like she was an idiot. It took much restraint to remind myself that she was phenomenal in bed and was willing to show me her pussy at the club. Otherwise I would have told that dumb bitch to kick rocks.

"What do you mean, which part, Zelda?"

"That's not funny. What's an ode? I don't get it. I heard 'dry hump' and 'clit.'"

"Forget it. The point is; I'm writing a book."

"For what? Listen, I called because I got tickets to come and see you with the money I won."

"Why don't you pay your bills off first and then come see me."

"I did."

"No Zelda, I mean like pay three months in advance, so you don't have to worry for a while."

Our conversation seamlessly blended from being responsible with her money to something vulgar and sexual.

Within minutes of finally hanging up, Private Marche, my easy listening station, text messaged me her request to stay the weekend. She was a welcome relief from everything that was going on in my life. By the time she arrived on Friday evening, I was well into thirty handwritten pages of an autobiography. She encouraged me to use her computer for the next week to help the creative process.

That's all I needed to become dedicated to the cause. My butt was glued to the wooden chair in my room, which was laden with several pillows and two blankets. I became a recluse, perfectly content listening to the same song on repeat for six and a half hours. My breaks were utilized to urinate and perform a deep groin stretch when my ass went numb. Food was delivered and eaten as I typed and stared at the blinking cursor on the screen. The focus was pure and somewhat animalistic. Like how a lioness must become when she zeroes in on her kill at a watering hole.

My story didn't need to be told; it had to be told. I felt compelled and convinced this book was my calling.

Unbeknownst to me, a week had passed by the time Marche visited again. Excitedly, we scrolled through pages of text to exploit the work I had been committed to while she was training.

"Can I read it?" she asked. Her interest made me proud as she read my unedited draft. Her facial expressions morphed through each emotion. She giggled out loud a few times, smirked a lot, and then her face went serious before she finally finished

Unashamed

with a soft sigh. "It's good. I want to read more. It kind of made me horny."

With laughter and delight, I bounced on the corner of the bed. "Would you buy it?"

"Yes, I'd buy it." She swirled around in the shitty computer chair to face me.

"Good. So, you're horny huh? Maybe we can fix that." She caught my suggestion without hesitation. Marche was becoming less timid with each sexual encounter. The dynamic was certainly getting stronger, but the chemistry with Zelda far surpassed what Marche was able to bring.

Infatuation is an understatement when it came to Zelda. It was more like one hundred percent in lust. Her visit was less than memorable, but we shared some good times before her return to Vegas. Her presence lingered beyond her stay and became a nuisance to my friendships. She was the topic of every conversation because I was still in heat, a Zelda-heat, days after she left. Mandy and Marche suffered through each idolizing speech about her with glazed, disinterested eyes.

In a last ditch effort to gain my undivided attention, Marche asked me to take her out for her twenty-first birthday.

Private Marche, try as she might, could not match the heavy drinking standards to which Mandy and I were accustomed. Her attempts to match our shots ended in a parking lot vomiting session as we waited for our cab to arrive.

She crawled onto my lap and rested her head on my shoulder as the driver shot me a warning look from the rearview mirror. I rubbed her back, occasionally kissed her forehead, and hummed a song the entire trip back to the barracks. She apologized the next morning on the phone and was quite upset that the last night we shared together was wasted in a drunken stupor. "I just wanted to be with you one more time before I went back to Illinois." Her voice was tired and scratching at my ear through the phone.

"You had fun, right? That's what twenty-first birthdays are for!"

I heard a smile through her attempts to lick her lips. "I really did. I had so much fun with you, thank you. I just… wanted to be with you and I fucked it up."

"Aw, I'll miss you 'squishy.' Remember to go forth and be bold! Don't let any more women walk all over you."

Marche laughed at the nickname. "Got it. I'll miss you too."

We said our goodbyes and Private Marche returned to her home state the next afternoon.

We'd met at a crossroads where I needed her as much as she needed me to teach her independence. Giving her advice was easy. Following my own words of wisdom would prove to be more challenging.

Chapter 14

In the week prior to my return home, my nerves unsettled me into a constant state of nausea. My stomach was constantly churning with worry and anxiety, and it became difficult to eat.

Zelda, Douglas, and Patty called daily with questions about flight information and to ask about my general well-being because they loved me. I'm afraid. However, this description oversimplifies things. It doesn't register as a problem until you realize that this was a minimum of three separate phone calls typically lasting thirty minutes apiece which would have been fine had they left it at that. But it was multiple calls from each individual person who just wanted to chat, verify flight details, or simply say goodnight. Between the truth that needed to be told and the calls, my anxiety level peaked for the entire seven days. Guilt over everything weighed heavy on my shoulders. I prayed for an impossible prayer to be answered; more time.

I don't blame any of them though. It had been six months since I'd left Las Vegas, so naturally, they were excited for me to return home.

When I told Doug that my intention was to spend my first few days in Vegas with Zelda, he was beside himself. If that wasn't disgraceful enough, I asked him not to say anything to Patty. She was expecting me a few days later and didn't even know I was in town. Doug was deeply disturbed by all of it.

"What are you doing, Janell?" He questioned. "This is so stupid. I told you to get your shit together."

"I know. I just can't come home right away. I'm sorry." My voice was sheepish and guilt-ridden, but I didn't know what else to do.

Zelda received me at the airport. Not my husband of nine years or my girlfriend of two and a half. Even after returning to the city of sin, I couldn't bring myself, to be honest. In my brain, prolonging the inevitable justified a few more days of critical thinking. I was right, but it wasn't the kind of productive thought process I needed. It was mindless conversations with Zelda and meaningless sex which was just another procrastination tactic.

After two nights Zelda took me to a designated parking lot where I'd pre-arranged a ride home with Douglas. She argued with me the entire ride there.

"You can't keep doing this shit. You have a husband, a girlfriend, and me! Where the fuck do I fit in and how do you think this shit makes me feel? I'm sick of all this sneaking around. I don't deserve this!" She yelled while trying to drive safely by over-correcting with the steering wheel.

"I know, Zelda. I'm going through some fucked up shit right now, and I'm trying to figure it out." My eyes and head sulked to the floor. Truth be told I didn't care about anyone but Doug and how this was all going to play out for him.

"Figure what out? That you are a lesbian? I think they know! You just need to tell them and stop playing all of these games with people. I can't believe I'm dropping you off in a fucking parking lot so your husband can take you home to your *girlfriend*. Do you know how fucked that is?" She leaned her head on her hand that was supported by the driver's window after she parked in an empty space.

I didn't know what to say next but, luckily, I didn't have to speak at all because Doug was prompt as usual. Without inflection in my voice, I said, "That's him; I gotta go. I'll text you."

"Yeah, whenever you can sneak away. I'm always on hold, waiting for your call." She put the car in reverse to prepare for the moment I removed my last bag from her car. She was obviously not planning to stick around, and I couldn't blame her.

"I'll figure this out, Zelda." My assurance was all lies as far as she was concerned.

"Whatever. You sure know how to fuck with people's minds."

I certainly deserved that and felt myself sink into the strange realization of an oncoming depression. Or was it ongoing? I grabbed my luggage and rolled it through the parking lot to the back of Doug's car where he welcomed me and loaded my bags. Zelda quickly left before she had to see me greet him with a hug and a kiss on the cheek. I think she knew that it was over between us and that the past two days had been an escape from everything and that this was our unofficial goodbye.

It was awkward at first, but after a mile into our ride home, we started to reconnect. The famous Vegas skyline passed as we chatted with a little more ease. Doug stopped for gas as I sat in the passenger seat staring out of the window, contemplating my life. My head was swirling as if it was drunk with lies. There was nowhere for me to hide anymore; the time had come. I wondered when the right moment would present itself. Maybe when the day blows over, we can have a heart to heart conversation, and I can come out of the closet as quickly as I had on the phone with my family.

After a quick stop for gas, Douglas returned to the car. He began telling me a funny story as we made our way to the main road. I laughed at the things he was saying until he finished and I did a stupid and terrible thing.

"…then I told her about my 'lesbian' roommate like you are gay or something… if she only knew…" He snickered completely unaware of the turmoil in my head.

Without warning, words fell out of my mouth like verbal diarrhea. "I don't think you know how gay I really am." It was unedited, without thought and absolutely no censoring or regard for how it sounded. The words just spilled from my lips, and once they were out, I froze.

His eyes searched mine for the punch-line of a joke, but all he saw was conviction and sincerity. We held each other's stare for what seemed like an eternity then, when it seemed like the awkward moment couldn't get any more uncomfortable, the light turned red as if Jesus Christ himself was shocked at what I had done. It forced us to stop and have separate unspeakable thoughts mere feet from one another. We were trapped in the car and trapped within our individual minds. It was indescribable tension, unlike anything I have ever experienced.

With one shameful, mind-blowing, and insensitive sentence I tactlessly and accidentally came out of the closet to my husband. This was not how it was supposed to happen. Inwardly I cringed at how thoughtless I was. Had I been able to slam my head into the dashboard before me without humiliating myself further, I would have.

Gradually, fierce pains began to spread all over my body. It felt physical, but they were psychosomatic. My brain hurt, but it wasn't a headache. My chest hurt, but there was no clog. My breathing felt laborious, but I didn't suffer from asthma. I physically felt the pains because I had hurt the one person I loved most. Succumbing to emotions that I didn't even know existed was the result of the battle between my psyche and the venom that spewed from my mouth so carelessly. Blood exploded through my veins as fear of an unknown future possessed me. Then, my body became utterly exhausted as it gave up and shut down in an attempt to be numb. It felt as though the burst of emotions damaged the wiring in my body rendering me unable to function. The only thing I desired in that moment was death. I was ready to surrender myself to God.

Then the light turned green.

The Lord has a funny way of telling us that this too shall pass. The next fifteen miles was a blur, and the next thing I actually remember was walking behind Doug as we shuffled aimlessly up the stairs to Patty's room.

"Honey, I'm home!" Doug yelled as usual. It was amazing how he was able to keep things together following the biggest verbal shit-storm. I guess he was numb as he processed everything. He entered Patty's room first as if the world was spinning like any other day. But every movement was heartbreak, and every sound from his mouth was crying. We had been together too long and when a person you've shared everything with, built dreams with, has an emotional break – you know. I most definitely knew.

"Hi, baby, surprise," I said simply, without exclamation. Patty turned from her computer chair and sat in shock for a minute, then looked to Doug and back to me again.

"Oh my God. When did you get in?" Without moving her fingers from the keyboard, she remained seated as she asked both of us the question. The atmosphere in the room was extremely stale. In addition to Doug hiding his pain the best way he knew how, her reaction to my presence was less than enthusiastic; in fact, she never moved her fingers from the home keys.

"Doug picked me up. I wanted to surprise you." The lies I told made a sickness rush through my veins once again.

"You shits. I thought something was fishy. Come here baby; I've missed you." Patty rotated the computer chair in my direction and opened her arms for me. We hugged and kissed as I fell into her warm, comforting embrace where I lingered longer than I deserved. It was a shameful place for me to want to be.

Once the hug finished, she was a little over the top with excitement from a festival she and Douglas attended with two other women; one of which was Doug's current girlfriend. This excitement actually got her out of the chair so she could encourage me to see pictures they snapped. Doug seemed to have put up a wall because he relaxed and cracked a few jokes during my review of each photo. His ability to shut down emotionally amazed me. I envied his gift and secretly wished I could do the same.

Patty remained in this ring of happiness as she explained the outstanding concerts and the debauchery they experienced together. Doug participated in the exaggerated storytelling complete with high pitched laughs and fond explanations of memories. Perhaps, I thought, he doesn't think I'm serious about being a lesbian. While mulling over a thousand little crazies in my head as my husband and girlfriend hovered over me, a fascinating fact became clear. Patty's 'friend' in the photos was her mistress. The saying, "pictures say a thousand words" is an understatement. I was totally shocked that she would cheat on me, but considering the circumstances, my mouth was sealed. Despite my own infidelities and conflicted opinions about the stability of our relationship, it really hurt my fucking feelings.

Touché, my darling freckle-faced lover. You got me.

During a pause in awkward conversation I said, "Oh guys, I'm going to write a book. I've already started. Do you want to read what I wrote so far?" I began digging in my luggage for the storage drive that held my rough draft.

"What!" Patty exclaimed as if she actually cared. It was a good theatrical effort though.

"You are?" Douglas crossed his arms over his chest and tilted his head. I was unsure how to read that gesture considering the previous chain of unfortunate events.

"What's it about?" She asked with a minute level of interest as she continued to click through a few more photos on the computer.

"My life." I handed her the device. She pushed it into her computer's USB port as the three of us stood around waiting for it to load. When it did, she read the first few lines out loud. That's when she finally took it seriously and with more interest.

"*Ode to the mighty dry hump!* What the fuck, you're a dork. *The Godsend to any little girl's clitoral repertoire.* Ha! That's funny!" Her genuine excitement finally expelled which made me smile.

Patty and Doug laughed loudly. They always understood my humor. After a few pages, Douglas excused himself to retire, claiming he didn't want to read any more until it was finished. Patty read the first few pages and closed the program because she too would wait until it was done. "I want to read... you." She grabbed me and tried to get frisky.

"I can't. I'm going to sleep with Doug tonight." My arms gently pushed her away.

"What the fuck, why?"

"Because I just came out of the closet and he is fucked up right now." I tried to whisper and be heard at the same time.

Patty's hands immediately went to her mouth muffling her words as she spoke. "What? When, in the car? Oh my God, is he okay?"

"Hell no, he isn't okay." I tried to hush my tone. "I just flipped his entire world upside down, so I'm going to sleep with him tonight, all right?"

"Fine. I love you, baby; everything is going to be okay." She gave me a genuine hug, releasing some of the tension trapped in my body.

"I love you too and, no, it really isn't. I just ended nine years of marriage in the most fucked up way possible. Give us some time." We kissed each other before I walked out into the cold and uninviting hallway. I took a breath before opening his door.

In my husband's clean and perfectly organized room, I shamefully undressed and climbed into bed without saying a word. It was painfully awkward. For a while, we lay together uncomfortably numb. My eyes swirled as I looked into the darkness. For the first time in our lives, we were at a loss for words. I'm sure each of us opened our mouths in an attempt to speak but hesitated and decided against it. I know I did. Finally, when hiding the way that we felt about the situation couldn't be buried any longer we lost all composure and cried.

I faced my wall, and he faced his; our backs inches from the comforting warmth of the one another. We remained in this position trying desperately to stop weeping; futile in our attempts. If one calmed for a moment, it only took the others irregular breathing to reset the vicious cycle of heartbreak. Each of us tried desperately not to hyperventilate. We flooded ourselves in rivers of tears, frozen with the question of what to do next.

Unashamed

He was the first to make a move as I was too afraid to. He rolled over, grabbed me, and pulled me tightly into his arms. I twisted around to return his squeeze. As we wrapped ourselves in the other's embrace, our pain rekindled, and the tears once again flowed uncontrollably.

All we could do was sob until our eyes began to burn. The top portion of our expensive comforter was saturated with mucus and tears. This was absolutely the most deeply connected, emotional moment of our entire marriage. We cried ourselves into a pit of exhaustion and fell to sleep intertwined in one another's embrace.

The next two nights we were only able to manage a few words to each other, but bedtime always ended in the same way. Words expressed nothing the way tears did.

For those of us who have truly loved; the hardest thing to do… is walk away.

Chapter 15

After you tell your spouse that you are gay, what is the next step? Where are the how-to books on this subject? We were confused and depressed, but we were managing by coping in our own ways and collectively when possible. Couples handle things very differently, and, despite everything, Doug and I were maturely and responsibly dealing with the process together. The day we decided to go through our assets felt like we were being proactive in our separation and it oddly helped us push forward. Had we continued at our own pace, things would have been much easier, but Patty changed that. She thought I was leaving Doug to be with her... au contraire.

When I revealed the fact that I wanted to be alone, she exploded in anger. She let it be known that I was making the biggest mistake of my life with an excess of loud screams and over the top hand gestures. She would not stand for my rejection the way Doug had and even shamed me for the treatment I gave him over the past few years. She said anything she could think of to hurt me the way I was hurting her. When I wouldn't bend on my decision to leave both of them, she immediately expected me out of the house by the fifteenth of the month; a specific date that she yelled several times so it would be crystal clear.

The fifteenth of the month was a whopping two weeks from the berating conversation. It was also a rotten time to explain that it would take longer than two weeks to find a place, but it had to be said.

Believe me; she let me know that she didn't give a shit by screaming at the top of her lungs. "THE FIFTEENTH!"

I respectfully turned from her room, tucked my tail in, and slept on the couch.

Coming out of the closet is the biggest suck-tastic adventure a person can know. Everyone reacts differently to the news. Some reactions you expect and some you don't. The consequences thereafter are also a hot, shitty mess that no one prepares you for; like living in the most awkward arrangement with an ex-husband and ex-girlfriend while searching for a rental of your own. But this situation was unique because rather than affecting one person, or my partner I was destroying a third person. Not to mention all of the family members involved who were dealing with this in their own way. The house that I built had fallen, and it was my fault. But these were the consequences of my actions, and there was nothing to do but to own them. This is the price I paid for becoming my truth.

In the beginning, it looked a lot like depression, because it was. It's the death of your old world and the birth of a new one which one would think is exciting but not when you deal with it alone. What do you do when said baby world shits on you for the first time? What then is there to do but lay it on your chest as you cry yourself to sleep so you can struggle through the next day?

For a while, I drank myself numb. It felt easier to cope with a little help from a bottle. In sober moments I numbed myself by fixating on mundane objects. I relied on them to transcend me into a deadened mindset. The revolving ceiling fan above my bed was self-soothing therapy. The blades rotated on the slowest setting were just enough for my eyes to catch one spin around on its center axis. The fan had the most mesmerizing, catatonic-inducing effect on a girl who only wanted to escape thoughts.

Luckily when I reached out to my family for help, they were there. My sister who was and always will be a constant supporter of the person I am offered calls whenever she could to check on me. Not everyone can say that, so I understand how profound this is. My dad helped me move out of the house and tried to be there for me, but he didn't know exactly what to do. Not that it mattered because he came, showed his face, gave me hugs and tried to simply be in my presence. We talked about coming out of the closet, but it was very general. He didn't understand it, but that's alright because general conversation and trying to comprehend is a starting point.

After my dad flew back to Ohio and I was alone again in my new place I found myself chained to my reflection in the mirror of a life unknown. I watched tears fall down my face as a change began to occur within my precious waves of conscious stability. Even in the thick of my emotional mayhem, it was clear that the only person who could pull me out of the fear from the world was me. But it began with pain and blame. Looking at myself, I cried big ugly tears and hit the bathroom countertops of my new place with my fists. Bam! I told you in eighth grade. Bam! I told you. And fuck you. Bam! I said it on the phone that it wasn't a phase. Am I right or am I right? Bam! I told you on the way to get our license, and god damn it, four years later I said it again. Bam! I've been saying it over and over, and you weren't fucking listening. That's when I sobbed and leaned over the sink and just let the tears and snot fall down the drain until I was exhausted. My fists, my chest, my heart, my everything hurt. When I finally stopped crying, I lifted my head and grabbed a hand towel to wipe my swollen face. That's when it hit me. I looked at my reflection again and stopped blaming everyone else. "No Janell. *You* weren't listening to yourself."

And that was my ah-ha moment of coming out of the closet and being unashamed.

Epilogue

Angel is happily married to a wonderful man, and together they run a successful business.

Sunny married her high school sweetheart, and together they have four children.

Robert has one child.

Kay has two children and has since remarried, twice.

Natalia is on her second marriage with three children. She told me to make her sound sexy in this book.

Monica was in a terrible motorcycle accident, but by the grace of God, survived and last I knew she was sober.

Tracy had her legal twenty-first birthday a few years after our break up, which would have made her seventeen at the time we dated, unbeknownst to me. On a trip to Las Vegas, I swear I saw an Oompa Loompa reflection in a shop window. When I turned to look, it scampered away with a slight waddle.

Lindsey (or "April?") moved to another state and continued to meet green-eyed women online. I wouldn't be surprised if she has a new address book.

Joy lives in Las Vegas and has since established herself in the music industry. She laughed hysterically when she read this book.

Rayya lives in Las Vegas and is an advocate for childhood cancer awareness, but she's still absolutely crazy.

Zelda is married.

Private Marche has been with her partner for many years.

Mandy runs her own business and rides a Harley.

Patty is a special education teacher with two children.

Doug is happily remarried with two children.

About the Author

Emma Janson is the non de plume of Janell who wrote the original book while serving in the United States Army at a time when there were implemented policies restricting gays in the military. She finished Unashamed after serving in Iraq and Afghanistan. Unashamed is her first published book and was written in with a direct style. The author has opted to preserve the language of her youth in this second edition.

Made in the USA
Middletown, DE
22 November 2019